Gerd Ludwig

Fun and Games with Your Dog

Expert advice on a variety of activities for you and your pet

Color photos by Christine Steimer
Drawings by Renate Holzner

Translated by Kathleen Luft

Consulting Editors: Dan Rice, D.V.M.
Palika

D1316855

BARRON'S

Contents

Preceding double spread: Dogs are able to let off steam when playing Frisbee.

Whether indoors, in the yard, or in open country, ball games are among a dog's favorite pastimes.

Preface

Play: Some people think engaging in games or sports is a waste of time, while others see recreational activities as a pleasant hobby. Rarely, however, is play central in our life. But seen through the eyes of a dog, things look entirely different—dogs play to occupy themselves, and as they play, they develop coordination and strength and learn to explore their surroundings. Playing is an essential step on the dog's path to physical and mental maturity. For the pet owner, the dog's desire to play is an ideal basis for teaching it the fundamentals of obedience and for keeping it physically and mentally fit through various forms of training and "mental exercise."

This Barron's pet owner's manual will show you how to offer your dog a new, full life through games and sports. When you take the breed personality test, you will learn what your pet's particular aptitudes are. Tips from a veterinarian and a feeding plan for active dogs also provide valuable information.

The HOW-TO pages present the entire range of sports and games for play in your house or apartment, in your yard, and away from the house. A special chapter is devoted to sports available through clubs and to Agility competition.

The action-filled color photos were taken by Christine Steimer; the informative drawings are the work of Renate Holzner. This Barron's pet owner's manual is intended for all owners who want to keep their dog healthy and fit and to share more fun and games with their pet.

The author of this book and the editors of Barron's books wish you a great deal of pleasure as you play with your dog.

Please read the "Important Note" on page 63.

Playing Makes Dogs Happy

The Model: The Wolf, the Dog's Ancestor

Even today, dogs continue to display many similarities to their ancestors—the wolves. Anyone who has studied their way of life closely is aware that most of the dog's behavior is traceable to its wild heritage. This book deals with ways to play and share activities with a canine companion. A brief look at the wolf family will show how important play is for the healthy physical and mental development of a dog. Even more intensively than their domesticated descendants, wolf parents devotedly attend to the upbringing of their offspring. Most canine behavioral traits and habits are indelibly imprinted on puppies' personalities between three and twelve weeks of age. During this imprinting phase, or until about the eighth week of life, the wolf pups enjoy a "baby bonus" that allows them to do many things that later on are absolutely forbidden or greatly disapproved of in the orderly social system of the wolf. The magic word of the little wolves' taboo-free childhood is "play." Without fear of punishment the young are allowed to fight over food and to divide up the roles of hunter and quarry. They play tracking games and practice repelling an enemy or making a hasty retreat. The pup's play even includes precocious imitations of courtship and mating rituals.

Learning Life's Lessons through Play

Play is vital for young wolves and young dogs. Only at play can they become acquainted with their surroundings and fathom the finely tuned network of relationships within the family. Play teaches the laws of the wolf pack and tests the animals' capabilities. They learn as they play, and little by little they are accepted into adult society and familiarized with the duties and responsibilities that lie ahead.

As adults, both wolves and dogs use play as a way to test their rank within the order of the pack, to try new experiences, and to grapple with changes in their living conditions.

New Duties

On the long path dog and man have traveled as partners, the dog has been a friend and companion, a valuable helper, a herder and protector of the flocks, a guardian, an ally in the hunt, a pack animal, and a draft animal. We humans selected and bred the dogs we deemed well suited to these tasks. Today, however, working dogs are in the minority. We ask a family dog to do very little these days. Countless dogs that lead inactive lives suffer from boredom and would welcome duties and challenges. Dogs need something to do! Without activity, they develop bad habits and tend to misbehave.

If you keep your dog occupied by playing and exercising with it on a regular basis, you will develop a partner that keenly enjoys life and is mentally alert.

Before you start our program of play and training, test to see which sports and games are most suitable for your pet—and most enjoyable for both you and your dog.

Retrievers, like all dogs, still possess the characteristics of their ancestor, the wolf.

Jumping through a tire is an exercise that is especially fun for experienced athletes.

What Dogs Can Do

Different Attributes

The most obvious differences among the more than 400 dog breeds officially recognized today are variations in size, coat color, and coat structure. Breeders, however, began quite early to focus special attention on certain abilities and character traits in their animals. There are, for example, dogs with marked herding instinct, such as collies and Swiss mountain herd dogs. Other dogs take great pleasure in the hunt, such as retrievers and dachshunds.

If you bear in mind the particular abilities of your dog, and its individual preferences, you will have less trouble and enjoy greater training success. If you select appropriate games and sports for your dog, it will participate with enthusiasm and endurance (see Personality Test, page 7).

Before You Start Training

This book does not contain detailed information about housetraining your pet, nor do I discuss basic leash-training exercises. Those omissions aren't meant to imply that such training is not important; it is assumed that you will begin housebreaking your pet immediately after you get the dog. You will give it a great deal of time outside in your yard, take it for walks regularly, and praise it when it uses designated areas for its natural eliminations.

We also assume that you will begin the puppy's leash training immediately by fitting it with a lightweight leather collar. Short walks on the leash should begin within a few days, using a treat or toy to prevent it from balking. When produced, the leash should elicit excitement and joy from the dog. A collar and leash should *never* be used as a means of punishing the pet, but should be employed to enforce verbal commands and establish human control and gentle dominance over the dog.

It goes without saying that all dogs should be made to behave in automobiles. Whether traveling a few blocks to the park or a long distance, car manners are critical. To keep the dog in its designated area, fasten its short leash to a seat belt. You can also purchase a seat belt harness for your pet, just for car trips.

Before training begins, a critically important aspect of dog ownership is your responsibility for the dog's general health. Conscientious owners will take their new pets directly to their veterinarians. They will confer with their veterinarians about necessary vaccinations, worm checks, heartworm prevention, external parasite control, and other preventive care programs. Vaccinations are crucial for puppies at about six to eight weeks of age, followed by boosters a few weeks later. No pups should be allowed contact with strangers or other dogs until they have been properly immunized. Annual physical examinations should be scheduled, concurrent with booster vaccinations. With modern preventive care programs, your dog can live a long, happy, and healthy life.

This spaniel carefully follows a scent.

Personality Test

Do You Know Your Dog?

"Of course I know my own dog!" you will counter indignantly. And you will be right. You certainly see your pet more frequently and know its personality better than anyone else. Sometimes, however, emotional closeness and long years of sharing a household can interfere with objective judgment. The truth is that owner and dog subconsciously play long-familiar roles. If both parties are content with their roles in the relationship, there is no reason for change. If, however, you would like to put some zip into the daily routine by introducing new experiences, new activities, and new tricks, you will do well to ask yourself: What is my dog really like? To avoid problems from the very beginning, you should decide what to expect from your dog, where added emphasis is called for, and where a gentle approach is in order.

Canine Personality Types

Dominant and self-assured. These dogs are a challenge. Often you can recognize a future boss while it is still in its puppy basket—fearless, demanding, and always the first to do something. Adult unneutered males are most likely to advance their claims in clear body language. Dominant dogs are more difficult to train than others, and consistency, together with a firm hand of authority, is essential in their rearing. When playing, make sure that the dog does not use what it supposes to be freedom of action to test the rank order. Competitive games (chasing a ball, playing tug-of-war) have to follow fixed rules at all times; the dog *must* let go whenever told to do so, and it has to begin and end the game on command. If it snaps or growls menacingly, stop the game at once.

Timid, shy, or fearful: These dogs need experienced trainers. A sharp command voice is taboo, but a constantly stroking hand can be equally wrong. Some dogs are born opportunists and use their shyness quite consciously. The timid dog often knows very well what it wants, and usually achieves its goal more easily than its more confident fellows. Playing together is the correct method of strengthening the self-confidence of a fearful pet. The dog will gain self-assurance through playing games that require agility, such as ones that involve seeking, retrieving, or competing. Start with simple exercises that your pet can master quickly.

Now brave, now fainthearted. Most dogs are neither Rambos nor cowards. Depending on the situation, they either react valiantly or keep their distance. You should exhibit the same flexibility when participating in sports or games. If your four-legged partner is confused by being asked to perform unaccustomed tasks, simplify the exercise. If the dog acts bored or disinterested, incorporate new incentives.

Note: Regardless of your dog's type, you, as the "boss of the pack," should always determine the beginning, length, and end of the daily play session. Naturally, you should evaluate your pet's attitude on a particular day, and determine whether it is in a mood to play. Fixed times for play will ensure that your dog does not besiege you with its ball and Frisbee around the clock, or scratch at the door and whine to "persuade" you to go jogging. Between play sessions, store the toys and sports equipment where the dog cannot see them.

Profiles of Breed Groups

Terriers: These former harriers (rabbit dogs) and gun dogs have lost nothing of their self-confidence, high spirits, and courage. Keenly alert and highly active, they often are too restless for indoor sports and games. Outdoors they are eager to play rigorous, energetic games—anything from ball games to Frisbee (see page 44). Their innate fierceness should not be encouraged by playing fighting games. They should not be rewarded with treats too often; as small terrier breeds put on weight quickly.

Herding and working dogs: These include Australian cattle dogs, collies, Old English sheepdogs, Bernese mountain dogs, German shepherd dogs, and Border collies, among others. Those breeds, and virtually all sporting dog breeds, enjoy retrieving games. Most of them are fine swimmers, and all thrive on athletic activities that involve agility, fetching, seeking, and hiding. Choose games that stimulate their mental faculties and keep them busy for extended periods. A human partner should be present at all times.

Sight hounds: These dogs, such as greyhounds and whippets, are happiest when trying to outrun the wind. The best activities for them are those that build and maintain endurance, such as running or jogging with you or running on a leash alongside your bicycle. Following scents and testing their agility, on the other hand, are less suitable exercises for them.

Scent hounds and sporting dogs: Basset hounds, beagles, retrievers, and spaniels are correctly believed to have great scenting ability. Their favorite games are those that feature using their noses seeking objects.

Companion dogs: Dalmatians, poodles, and miniature schnauzers are wonderful family dogs, and you can excite their enthusiasm for any physical fitness program that requires a partner, including Agility (see page 54).

Small dogs: Chihuahuas, Pomeranians, Maltese, Shih Tzus, papillons, and Pekingese are agile and bright. Ideal for them are games that require mental effort or agility, hide-and-seek games, and cuddling games—outdoors or indoors.

Watch dogs and guard dogs: Boxers, rottweilers, Dobermans, and other aggressive breeds learn very quickly and will join in any kind of fun and games. If their strong protective instinct is encouraged, however, they will defend everything against everybody.

Tips from the Veterinarian

Your dog should be examined prior to beginning vigorous athletic activities. Periodic, complete physical examinations, performed by a veterinarian, are essential parts of all rigorous training schedules.

Congenital, Developmental Bone Diseases

Dogs that walk with arched backs, or those that limp and are obviously in pain, may be suffering from bone diseases. A veterinarian can diagnose the condition by physical examination, aided by X rays or ultrasound imaging.

Except for traumatic injuries, the most common skeletal problems are developmental disorders of the elbows, hips, stifles (knees), and shoulders. Joint inflammation may require medications or immobilization of the affected leg. In either case, physical activity should be curtailed during recuperation, and your veterinarian's advice should be followed carefully. If a serious bone or joint deformity exists, surgical intervention may be required to permanently correct the condition.

Breeds of dogs that have a tendency to develop skeletal problems should not be subjected to too much stress. Games that require going all out are not really suitable for them.

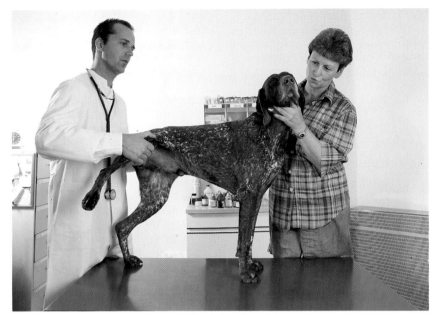

Large breeds need to be examined for skeletal problems.

Rest and Recuperation

In the following cases, sports and games must be stopped in order to allow healing to occur:
- after any surgical operation
- when bones are immobilized by splints or casts
- after the fifth week of pregnancy
- during any serious illness

Follow the veterinarian's advice regarding the length of time your dog should be rested in any of those instances.

Gentle Play: When and Why?

There are breed-related diseases that may necessitate play restrictions when symptoms are present.

Very small breeds such as Chihuahuas, Yorkshire terriers, and toy and miniature poodles are subject to hereditary stifle and hip deformities. Those congenital defects are often associated with kneecap dislocations and hip dysplasia.

Short-muzzled breeds such as English bulldogs, Boston terriers, pugs, and Pekingese often display breathing difficulties and choking seizures when excited, especially during hot weather.

Breeds Predisposed to Spinal Disease

Bassets, dachshunds, Pekingese, and springer spaniels are often at risk for prolapsed intervertebral discs. Moderate, controlled exercise in healthy dogs of those breeds may actually help prevent occurrence of the condition.

Large and Giant Breeds

Saint Bernards, Great Danes, German shepherd dogs, and most hunting breeds are prone to congenital hip and elbow dysplasia. Those hereditary diseases are manifested by deformed joints that predispose to arthritis and extreme dysfunction.

9

Older Dogs of All Breeds

Older dogs may show symptoms of heart or lung disease. During extreme excitement, they may even lose consciousness. Regular physical examinations should warn you of impending danger associated with exercise of your old pet.

Making Light Work of Training

The Right Training Program for Each Stage of Life

At every age, dogs display certain abilities and needs. A puppy wants to discover the world while its adult counterpart appreciates familiar surroundings. Older animals often withdraw and become more distant, trying in this way to conceal diminishing vitality.

Through basic and advanced training, you bring your own demands and ideas into harmony with those of your dog. Training doesn't end when you are finished schooling puppies and young dogs in the fundamentals. It also includes refresher training for full-grown dogs and gentle adapting of senior dogs to their changed world. Whatever your dog's age group, it is helpful to combine training with play.

Puppies: Play and a Little Training

Between the eighth and twelfth weeks of a puppy's life, it leaves the breeder to go to its new home. That means separation from its mother, siblings, and familiar people and surroundings. The puppy has already learned important rules of behavior from its mother. Its new owner needs to assume the role of "substitute mother" immediately, because it is precisely during this imprinting phase that the dog is particularly amenable to teaching. The lessons it learns at this early age will have a lasting influence on its life. It is not true that young dogs should be allowed to run rampant; from the very outset, they should be given small tasks and incentives that teach them through play.

Exploratory play: The owner and the puppy together search for hidden toys. Every find is rewarded immediately with petting, praise, or treats. The dog will become acquainted with its environment and lose its fear of the unfamiliar.

Competition: "Battling" over the puppy's cuddly blanket, a rope, or a rubber ring will strengthen its self-confidence and fitness.

Active games: By playing ball games, tag, and fetch, the puppy will become aware of and improve its physical abilities. At the same time it will work off excess energy and subliminal aggression.

Social games: Playful contact with strange humans, other dogs, and other pets will socialize the young dog, keep it from being afraid of being touched, and teach it "manners."

Make sure, however, that the puppy does not determine the course of the game. Objects that it has won also have to be relinquished on demand. If it refuses to do so, this means that it does not acknowledge its owner as "leader of the pack."

Young Dogs: Play after Every Training Session

Early training, including housebreaking your pet, teaching it to answer to its name, and getting it to accept the collar and leash, has already begun in puppyhood. This basic training phase will last another three to four months, during which time the young dog will become familiar with all the major commands. With a growing dog, games and toys make the training session more relaxed and serve as a reward for success. Commands such as

If you have an older dog, don't overtax it—old dogs should not try to compete with younger dogs.

"Come!" "Sit!" and "Down!" will be accepted more quickly if you motivate your pupil with its favorite toy or treat. Let the dog see the treat in your hand, but do not reward it until the exercise is finished. Interspersing the lessons with short games will ease the tension, and the dog will see that its cooperation is rewarded by being given a chance to play with you.

Adult Dogs: Encourage Participation through Play

In an intact animal-human relationship with correctly assigned roles, every dog wants to please its owner, the leader of its pack. But dogs are lazy by nature, and will try to attain the goal with the least possible effort and energy. Thus, over the years, a family dog becomes somewhat reluctant to follow directions or inclined to simply ignore them. Time for a refresher course! What is easy in light of the enthusiasm and curiosity of young dogs often degenerates into hard work with adult dogs. The magic motivator is play, and after all the years they have spent together, owners certainly know exactly which games have an especially great influence on their pets.

Older Dogs: Play Keeps Them Young Longer

With dogs over the age of eight, training is not of prime importance, although older dogs are precisely the ones that need to follow the basic commands without complaining. That is especially true of aging males, since they often become more obstinate and intolerant of their surroundings. Obviously, this is their way of trying to conceal the visible signs of aging. With games that ensure the older dog a reasonable probability of success, you can bolster their impaired self-confidence. Just as with a puppy, praise, rewards, and petting are

Playing boisterously with other dogs is an important experience for pups.

effective. It is important to shorten the usual play periods and set simple tasks that are easy to perform.

Keeping the Fun in Games

- No playing immediately after meals! This applies particularly to puppies and to large dogs, due to the danger of a life-threatening gastric torsion (see page 59).
- Do not allow the dog to defend its toys. It has to accept that all playthings belong to its owner.
- Give your dog only a few toys. Usually it will have a certain favorite toy anyway.
- Toys that squeak are popular with many dogs (ideal as a reward). You need to test the toy ahead of time, to see whether your own nerves can stand squeak-toy concerts. You should also check the toy to be sure the metal squeaker cannot be easily removed from the toy; they are sometimes swallowed, and can be dangerous.

Indoor Fun and Games

Many Ways to Have Fun

Playing indoors can be far more than a bad-weather alternative to training in the yard. For instance:
• Games in the house do not depend on good weather. They can be enjoyed regardless of rain, cold, or wind. In summer, you can play in cool rooms with dogs that are sensitive to heat.
• An indoor play area is visible at a glance and limited in size. It is ideal for dogs that have not yet been obedience trained, and run away when outdoors.
• Your physical proximity to the dog makes the initial obedience exercises easier.
• Exercises and training programs that demand concentration and deliberation can take place without distractions.
• The risk of overexertion and injury is lower in the house than outdoors.
• Often, an occasional short play session in the house is possible when there is not enough time for outdoor games and sports.
• Playing indoors is the only chance some dogs get for physical activity. This applies especially to puppies before their vaccinations are in full effect. Indoor exercise is vital for very old dogs or dogs with severe skeletal problems. Dogs that are not completely fit following an operation or an illness also may be exercised indoors.

The toy your puppy prefers can be a life-long favorite.

Puppies' World of Play

From the third week of life on, young dogs playfully try to "bite" and put their paws on the muzzles of their mother or littermates. With their tail wagging and their forequarters flattened to the ground, they issue an invitation to join in the fun. While at play, a puppy improves its reactions and motor coordination and develops individual initiative and courage. For a young dog, playing means gaining experience. When it joins your household at the age of eight to twelve weeks, it is in the midst of this explorer phase that shapes its entire life. You, as the new pack leader, need to arouse the dog's interest in games and physical activity from the very first day! Since the little creature is not protected against the most dangerous infectious diseases, such as distemper, until after its second series of shots (in the twelfth week of life), it should have no contact with other dogs before that time.

Playing with a puppy is always a kind of educational activity as well. The owner, as the pup's playmate, continues its training, taking the place of its mother and littermates.

Playful fighting and tussling makes early training and the initial grooming procedures easier to perform. You can simulate the typical behavior of adult dogs toward a puppy by placing your hand around the puppy's muzzle in the same way the mother corrects her puppy with a gentle bite on its muzzle. Placing your hands on its throat demonstrates your superiority. Turning the puppy over on its back also illustrates your dominance.

Now it's time to play; this owner can read later.

You should inspect its eyes, ears, and teeth on a regular basis. Practice combing and brushing as well, to get the puppy familiar with all the necessary grooming procedures early. Be gentle but firm when grooming, taking care not to stimulate defensiveness in the pup.

Hide-and-seek games are ideal for expanding the puppy's world during the first few days (see HOW-TO: Games to Play Indoors, page 18).

Games of fetch follow seeking games naturally. The puppy will learn to pick up objects, bring them back, and drop them in front of you (see page 18).

Ball games are a good way for young dogs to practice control of their body and reactions (see page 19).

Active games include races and chases, which help the dog perfect its control of body movements.

Caution: Before the puppy's motor coordination is well developed, be careful not to overtax your pet by asking it to run in a zigzag or to play running games on stairs.

Important: Don't play games that involve fighting over or tugging on a rope, a blanket, or an old sweater before your puppy has its new set of teeth (twentieth week); a broken tooth could permanently spoil its enjoyment of such games.

It is also important in puppy play to be aware of the following:

• As early as possible, teach your puppy not to bite your hands, legs, or clothing. If it bites during a game, turn it over on its back or give it a little pinch, following its mother's example, see page 12).

• Occasionally, the puppy will suddenly nod off in the middle of a boisterous game. If that happens, let your pet have its rest!

• To preserve the young dog's enthusiasm for play, never tire it or blunt its pleasure with endless repetitions.

Invitation to Participate in Play

The dog has a wide range of different behaviors that indicate it is in the mood for play:

• lowering the front part of its body to the ground, usually in combination with friendly wagging of its tail

• making the so-called "play face" with teeth bared, nose wrinkled, and eyes wide open, and a relaxed facial expression

• bringing its favorite toy and presenting it to you

• pretending to bite, either by gently nibbling at its partner in play or biting at the air several times

• nudging you with its muzzle

• seizing a play object (blanket) with its teeth and shaking it

• putting a paw on you

• "laughing," with upper lip raised and teeth bared

• giving a growl of invitation or barking loudly

The Right Way to Play

Constant exposure to stimuli causes the dog's motivation and pleasure in learning to decrease markedly.

• Especially with early training through games, you need to observe a limit of no more than three training units of five to ten minutes a day. Restricting the number of repetitions of each exercise will ensure that the material learned will be permanently retained.

• When dogs are asked by children to play during their phases of sleep and rest, they may react aggressively, and, if repeated, they will no longer enjoy playing.

• Some dogs get completely out of hand, especially with games involving tugging and tussling. To maintain control, when you end the game, give the command "Down!" and let the dog lie there for at least one minute.

• Some dogs continue to be overexcited even after the game is over. Always take such pets for a short walk to calm them down.

• If the dog displays undesirable behavior during the game, ignore its lapse at first, unless the behavior is aggressive. However, it is essential to repeat the exercise immediately afterward.

• If the dog wants to stop playing, recall it and allow it to end the game

The Right Toys

Toys for a dog should be made of all-natural materials; they can be found in pet stores or department stores. Never buy anything made of plastic or anything that has been painted, glued, or treated with chemicals.

Toys to chew are especially important for puppies. Use rawhide bones, hard dog biscuits, chew sticks, solid nylon bones, or solid rubber rings. Do not play with small objects that can be swallowed or with toys made of painted wood, metal, or soft synthetic fabrics. Your worn-out shoes also are in that category, because young dogs cannot tell old shoes that are all right to chew from new ones that are off-limits.

Balls are good for playing alone or with a partner. Hard rubber balls are ideal. They should be just large enough to fit between the dog's teeth, but too big to be swallowed. Approved for older puppies are tennis balls, but not Ping-Pong balls. When playing soccer games, the dog moves the ball with its muzzle. For that sport, use a large, lightweight ball.

Balls made of soft leather or plastic are not recommended, because they can be torn and the pieces could be swallowed.

A blanket to cuddle or play with often becomes the dog's inseparable companion.

Rawhide bones and toy animals that squeak are very popular items. Rawhide bones serve as toys: they also strengthen the masticatory muscles, especially in puppies getting their permanent teeth. Squeak toys have educational value for puppies, as they help them lose their fear of unaccustomed, loud noises while still young.

Caution: The rubber covering of squeak toys has to be sturdy enough to withstand the dog's sharp teeth; otherwise, there is a danger that the squeaking mechanism will be dislodged and swallowed (see page 11).

A box for toys: Playing should be something special for your dog, and the reward-based games played during the basic training phase should be effective. Special quality time with your dog will preserve its enjoyment of play for many years. Playing is another opportunity to quickly break it of bad habits. For a dog left home alone, being given a toy from the box is like receiving praise in advance. Right after the finish command with which you conclude each play session, the toys should be put into the box—except for your pet's special blanket and possibly a rawhide bone (but there should be limitations on its availability too, even for puppies). Together with the commands you use to signal the start and finish of play, the opening and closing of the box announce that the human is in sole charge of the game.

Important: If your dog is unwilling to give up a toy, don't start a tug-of-war over the object; competition for it will be viewed as a challenge. Instead, distract your pet with treats or a more interesting toy. At the same time, give the "Let go!" command. Praise your pet once it relinquishes the toy, and repeat the exercise several times. Fighting over a toy by several dogs should also be prohibited.

Appropriate Toys:
1) *rubber ring to pull on*
2) *ring to throw*
3) *rubber ball*
4) *cuddly blanket*
5) *squeak toy*
6) *rope to bite*
7) *bone to chew*
8) *rubber ball with knobs to chew*
9) *wooden dumbbell to fetch*

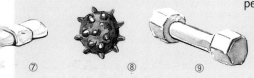

⑦   ⑧   ⑨

When they play "seek," experienced dogs can find hidden objects even under the sofa.

only after a concluding command ("Sit!" "Bark!" or "Give your paw!").

• Don't organize wild chases on a slippery floor or on stairs where there is danger of injury.

• Some toy breeds with a very light skeletal structure should never be induced to jump off a sofa or an armchair; bones of those delicate breeds are easily broken.

• In principle, do not play fighting games or tug-of-war with dominant dogs, especially males. Such competition tends to reinforce their self-confidence and leads to aggression.

It is important that you are the one who decides when and how long to play! Don't accept the dog's invitation right away—always give the "Sit!" or "Down!" command first; then give a signal that play can begin.

A Full Program

Although many indoor games are also suitable for outdoors, some are meant to be played only inside your home.

Games requiring thought and concentration: These promote and foster memory and should become part of your pet's recreational program during puppyhood.

• **Box game:** While your pet is watching, place a treat or a toy into one of two small boxes that differ in size, structure, or color. Then move the boxes around and direct the dog to search for the object. At first, leave the boxes open or loosely covered; later, for dexterity training, use boxes that the dog has to open.

• **Barrier:** Roll the ball underneath a barrier such as a railing. The dog will learn to reach its goal by a roundabout way (see page 18).

• **Tunnel test:** Tie a string to a toy and pull it through a tunnel about 3 feet (1 m) long, letting the dog see the toy disappear and reappear. Then leave the toy inside the tunnel. The dog will have to discover how to get the toy out again (see page 18).

• **String test:** Tie up your dog, and place a treat just out of its reach. With its paw, it should be able to reach a string tied to the object and pull the morsel close to it. This is a difficult challenge and should only be repeated a few times each session.

Hide-and-seek: Good things to hide are toys, scarves, or sweaters (not freshly washed), purses, or keyrings. Games of this kind should be started on your command and ended in a way that the dog can recognize easily. As a rule, seeking and retrieving the object constitutes a single training unit (see page 18).

Reminder: Don't use shoes as an object of your pet's search; the game can cause a dog to develop a habit of carrying off and chewing shoes!

Contact games and tussling: The range of these games extends all the way from the dog's giving you its paw to wrestling matches between human and dog. Contact games and tussling strengthen the partnership between owner and pet (see page 19). The human's role as leader of the pack has to be clearly established. Some dogs forget themselves rather quickly when measuring their strength against that of their owner, resulting in torn clothing or scratches. End every contact game quickly if the dog starts to bite, growl angrily, or bare its teeth aggressively. After the "Down and stay!" command, the dog should remain lying down for several minutes while you ignore it (see The Right Way to Play, page 14).

Playing alone: Playing is an ideal pastime for dogs that are home alone, and is the best way to curtail destructive habits caused by boredom. Playing alone, however, does not mean that the dog itself decides what and with which toys to play. Toys for solo play should be made available only for the time of the owner's absence; otherwise, the toys will quickly lose their attractiveness. Here's an example: While home alone, the dog is allowed to play with its hedgehog squeak toy, a ball, and a rawhide bone. As soon as its owner returns, these toys are put away. Dogs with a herding instinct can be given a guarding assignment in addition, such as guarding a purse.

Important: After every session, praise and pet your dog. Recognition from its master or mistress is a reward and a form of validation for the dog.

Treats that provide incentives during training give a dog proof that its owner is satisfied with it. Especially suitable are low-calorie snacks that help the dog keep its "figure."

This owner pulls a toy out of the basket as if by magic.

HOW-TO:
Games to Play Indoors

Hide-and-Seek Games

This is the perfect game for an indoor setting! Hide an object that is familiar to the dog, such as a toy, a piece of cloth, or—as an incentive during the initial attempts—a treat. If the dog has learned the "Sit and stay!" command, have it wait until the object is hidden. If not, have a second person hold the dog still until you release it with the "Find it!" command. At first, stay with the dog and signal the direction of search and the closeness of the hiding place by saying: "No! Not there!" or "Great! Right! Good dog!" The appropriate tone of voice will ensure that the dog makes the right connection. Start simply. With young dogs in particular, success and praise count far more than the degree of difficulty.

Level 1 (for very young puppies): Place the object on the floor in the same room as the dog, where it can see it. Start using the customary commands at this stage, even if the puppy doesn't know what to do yet.

Level 2: Hide the object in the next room, so that the dog can see it from the door.

Level 3: Place the object under a sofa or an armchair.

Level 4: Conceal the object on the floor under pillows or blankets, which the dog will have to push aside.

Level 5 (for experts): Put the object on a chair or in a basket or a coat pocket.

During repetitions, a dog generally will look in the places where previously it had found the object. Inexperienced dogs may be discouraged if you change the hiding place each time. Of course, you also can hide and have your dog hunt for you.

Games Requiring Thought and Dexterity

Drawings 1 and 2

Hide-and-seek: This game can be a kind of mental game in which the dog is shown an object whose appearance and scent it must remember in order to find it again. Well-hidden objects require a great deal of mental effort and deduction on the part of the dog, especially objects hidden under the rug, in boxes with or without lids, or lined up among similar objects. Long-term memory is tested when the dog is told to search for an object several hours or even a day after hiding it.

Games involving alternate routing require reorientation, a difficult job for a dog.

The barrier game: In this game, a ball is rolled through the gap under a wide board (or a stretched-out blanket). The dog cannot follow it directly, but has to go around the obstacle (see Drawing 1). Games of dexterity and reorientation that involve boxes lend themselves to a great many variations, depending on the kind of lid or fastening that has to be opened with the dog's paw or muzzle in order to find the reward.

The tunnel test: In this game, the dog watches while a toy or treat on a string is pulled through a tunnel approximately 3 feet (1 m) long. After several demonstrations, leave the object inside the tunnel (initially at the end of the tunnel, later in the middle as well). Encourage the dog to look for it (see Drawing 2).

Playing Fetch

It doesn't occur to a puppy to bring hidden objects and balls

1) A barrier: By making a detour, the dog reaches its goal.

2) The dog is supposed to bring an object out of the tunnel.

3) An empty hallway is ideal for the puppy's first ball games.

that have been thrown or rolled away back to its owner; instead, it will very likely drag its quarry off to a safe place. When that happens, take up your position near the spot where the puppy carried the object, usually its bed. If it brings the object to you, praise it in ingratiating tones. Repeat "Good dog!" Give the "Come!" command several times, and coax it to you. Then ask it to swap or trade the object it fetched for a treat, reinforcing the swap with the "Out!" command. If this works, shower your pet with praise. The prospect of something good to eat will induce it to return single-mindedly in subsequent attempts. After several repeated successes, move to another place. Later, have the dog take the sit position before you hand over the reward. If things do not go the way you wish, and if the dog doesn't

come back, or drops the object on the way, don't criticize or scold your pet, simply start the exercise again.

Ball Games
Drawing 3

When playing with a puppy, never throw, but roll, the ball toward the dog or away from it. The learning objective is to strengthen its motor coordination. Hard rubber balls, just the right size for your pet's mouth, are ideal. Balls to be tossed and caught by older dogs should be lightweight and thrown only from a short distance in the beginning.

Many dogs enjoy pushing or driving a ball for instance, a large ball such as a soccer ball is propelled forward by the dog's muzzle and feet. A long, narrow hallway that contains as little furniture as possible serves as a good site for preparatory training.

Contact Games and Tussling

The first games a dog learns are scuffling games that it plays with its littermates. Later, its owner assumes the important role of its partner in play. Never forget that you are the pack leader. Don't enter into activities that place your authority in jeopardy, such as wild fighting games in which the dog runs riot with excitement. As discussed on page 17, make sure that physical contact games are kept under your control. Always end every contact game with a finish command, such as "Sit!" If your pet

is especially excited, take it for a short walk on a leash to divert it.

Running and Jumping Games
Drawing 4

If you carefully watch your puppy on smooth floors, your house or apartment can also be used for action games. A tunnel of blankets can be set up quickly, and will help prevent your young dog from developing a fear of dark or enclosed places. Make the tunnel short at first, so that the puppy can readily see the exit.

To encourage your pet's initial attempts to jump, set up a hole in a doorway to jump through (see Drawing 4). Cut a circular hole in a sheet, and fasten the sheet to the doorframe with thumbtacks or Scotch tape. At first, the height of the jump should be only a few inches; later, raise the level. From the opposite side, hold out a treat to coax the dog to jump through the hole.

4) Jumping: A sheet with a hole in it substitutes for the tire.

Games in Your Yard

A Very Private Freedom

In your own yard you are free to do as you please. For your dog, your yard is also the promised land of small personal liberties where it wears no collar and leash and there's no need to heel or to maintain the down position for hours on end to keep from bothering its master and mistress.

Make Your Yard into a Canine Paradise

A fence or a wall is essential, to prevent the dog from expanding its playing field of its own accord. With young dogs in particular, the need for an enclosed yard is crucial.

The following trick will quickly teach your dog to respect the fence as a boundary: Attach tin cans to a string in a row, and hang them on the fence about 3 feet (1 m) above the ground. Usually, the clattering sounds of cans are sufficient to deter your pet from further attempts to jump or climb over the fence.

The lawn should definitely be part of your pet's play and sports area.

Flower and vegetable beds should be at the edge of the yard, or the dog will view them as an invitation to dig. It is important that every dog learn to distinguish between permissible and prohibited parts of the yard (see Taboo Areas, page 22).

Sources of danger, such as rabbit holes or garden tools left lying on the playing surface, should be eliminated.

This border collie proudly carries the big ball back to its owner, issuing an invitation to play again.

Many dogs view their owner's yard work as an invitation to play. They jump around the lawn mower, dig in the soil next to your hoe, and persist in biting at the unwinding coils of the garden hose. That may look comical, but it can be dangerous and should not be tolerated.

Make it a rule that your dog does not view yard work as a recreational interlude. Allow it to stay outdoors with you only if it behaves while you work.

Hedges and natural-stone walls offer small animals and birds a place to take cover and build nests. Make certain that your pet does not do any harm to them, especially during hatching season.

Soiling your lawn with feces can be avoided if you teach your dog that it has an obligation to notify you when nature calls, just as it does indoors. Then you can take it to its customary toilet area or assign it a spot in one corner of the yard.

Note: A healthy dog that is outdoors in all kinds of weather will seldom be totally clean when it returns to the house. After your puppy's first trip outside, acquaint it with the necessary clean-up procedures. A cloth or towel kept handy near the door will get the worst of the dirt off its belly and legs. In wet weather, follow up by rubbing your pet dry with a second cloth or towel. The dog should be trained to stand still, even when its sensitive feet are being wiped clean. To establish this habit, the procedure should be performed even on days when the dog is not dirty, to get it used to being rubbed off.

This curtain of brightly colored strips of fabric helps the dog overcome its fear of the unknown.

World of Wonders for Puppies

Most imprinting occurs between weaning and 16 weeks of age. Dogs that are trained and tested to perfect their natural talents during that developmental phase will have an advantage over others that you attempt to train at a later stage. At maturity, their early experiences will be reflected in their superior personalities—another reason for playing yard games with your puppy. In every case, puppy training exercises should be fun for the dog.

Touching games. Puppies should be taught to use all their sensory capacities to learn about their environment. In games involving touch, they become accustomed to different types of surfaces such as pavement, stones, plastic sheeting or tarpaulins, and surfaces that produce rustling noises, such as newspapers or foil. The narrow crosspieces of floor grates can press painfully into a dog's sensitive feet and they should not be asked to walk on them. At this point, puppies can also be introduced to preliminary water games in a shallow wading pool in your yard.

Other games of familiarization. Large, colorful balloons will frighten most young dogs at first, but, with training, the puppy will no longer flinch, even at the sound of balloons popping. Some pups even reveal themselves to be courageous "balloon killers" (see photo, page 64). In many professional dog schools, training and playing with large balloons is part of the basic training curriculum for family dogs after eight months of age. That training prevents dogs from becoming overly fearful of loud noises.

Other sound familiarization exercises include contact with tin cans. Tie empty cans to a rope and pull them across the path or sidewalk. Walking through a fabric tunnel made of blankets, and running through a rustling curtain made of plastic ribbons or strips of aluminum

Taboo Areas

Along with the grassy play area for the dog, your yard may also include roses you enjoy looking at, fruits and vegetables for the dinner table, or a compost heap for gardening. Under no circumstances should your dog dig up the roses, "water" the lettuce, burrow in the composted materials, or take a bath in the fish pond!

• Your dog should be taken for a walk regularly to relieve itself, or encouraged to use a corner of the yard set aside for that purpose. If your male dog insists on urinating on shrubs or trees, you can protect them with a 2-foot-high (61 cm) plastic sheath.

• If a dog is inclined to dig in the yard, provide a sandbox to dig in (see page 27). The sandbox should not be used as a toilet, however.

• A medium-high, portable plastic fence will keep flower and vegetable beds safe, at least while blooms and fruits are being produced. Sprays (available in pet stores) intended to keep dogs at a distance because of an unpleasant odor have little long-term effect and are quickly washed away by rain.

• Sharp gravel borders around beds and ponds often will have a permanent deterrent effect. The dog needs to step on it only once to get the message (see drawing, page 23).

• Always start games and sports far away from cultivated plants. When you and your pet play ball, keep your activities well away from the strawberry patch. If the dog persists in stepping on flowers, stop the game at once by saying "Sit!"

foil are also good exercises to help the puppy overcome its fear of noises (see HOW-TO: Games to Play in Your Yard, page 26, and photo, page 21).

Games involving recall and retrieval. Practicing "Come!" and "Retrieve!" in your yard is based on similar exercises indoors. In the yard, the tasks are more difficult due to larger surface areas, variations in terrain, and distraction by outdoor noises and smells. Let the dog run around on a long leash for a few minutes. Give the "Come!" command, in combination with the dog's name, and pull the leash toward you. If the dog responds, positive reinforcement is especially important. Give your pet a treat or its favorite toy, and let it play with it for a while. Soon the opportunity to play will be sufficient inducement, and the leash will become unnecessary. Never call "Come!" in order to punish the dog for a misdeed; the dog will relate the scolding to its return. Use a toy when you practice retrieving as well. With the dog on leash, hold its collar firmly and throw the toy a few yards. Then release the dog, under leash control, with the words "Fetch!" or "Bring!" If it picks up the object, call it back with the "Come!" command. Offer it a treat or another toy, and take the one it retrieved out of its mouth. With puppies in particular, the return is more likely to succeed if you squat down. You will seem smaller and thus far away, and the puppy will be in a hurry to get close to you again.

Note: To train retriever breeds, there are so-called dummies, intended to simulate the quarry. Game bird scents are also available to spray on the dummies to increase their attraction.

Outdoor games of hide-and-seek. Your yard offers new and fascinating opportunities for games of hide-and-seek, including tracking works, but think twice about hiding objects in

Surrounding a flowerbed with gravel will prevent your dog from trying to dig there.

the dirt. Puppies will interpret the chance to dig them out as blanket permission to dig wherever they like!

Outdoor Play for Everyone

For dogs whose physical development is complete, the following games are suitable.

Running and jumping: Few owners are inclined to exhaust themselves playing wild games of chase with their pet. One alternative is for two or three people to throw a ball to each other and send the dog from one position to another with the "Come!" command. Let the dog play with the ball briefly, to keep it from losing interest in the game (see page 26). Additional educational components are added by sending the dog away, saying "No!" when it goes to the wrong person, and praising it lavishly when it makes the right choice.

With a broomstick that will fall to the ground when touched (to prevent injury), you can easily set up a crossbar for your pet to jump over. Equally practical is a tire hung from a tree branch. Jumping through the tire requires more

In the photos: First, the dog balances a piece of cheese on its muzzle. At the command "Hup!" the dog tosses it into the air and catches it in its mouth.

Holding the piece of cheese on its muzzle . . .

. . . and throwing it into the air on command.

effort and body control than clearing the hurdle. At first, place the stick and the tire only a few inches off the ground. The dog's initial jumps should be little more than hops taken at a full run (see HOW-TO: Games to Play in Your Yard, page 26).

A word of warning: If a human plays the role of the "quarry" in a hot pursuit game, dominant dogs may misinterpret that as relinquishment of human authority.

Outdoor ball games: There is no official hit list of the most popular games to play outdoors with dogs; among the favorites, however, are games and sports involving balls. They include almost everything both master and pet are looking for. Anything goes—provided it is fun and has not been prohibited by your veterinarian (see Tips from the Veterinarian, page 8). Ideal toys are "biteproof" solid rub-

ber balls of the right size (see page 15). Experts recommend that you limit play with tennis balls because with extensive use, the fiber covering will eventually damage the teeth, as will rocks that some dogs love to retrieve.

In the game of ball-boxing (see also page 26), the dog dives for a larger ball that is thrown to it at medium height, and "boxes" it back to you with a vigorous thrust of its muzzle. Balls as light as possible—from hand size to no more than soccer-ball size—are the best choices. The dog should be trained to relinquish the ball on command.

Solo play with the ball should be allowed only under supervision, and the ball should be taken away after the play session. Their impulsiveness gets the better of many dogs when they play with a ball, and after a few minutes your flowerbeds may be included in the playing field.

Important: We repeat—never throw balls directly at the dog's face, and never play "catch" with balls the size of a golf ball. When your pet tries to catch a small ball, it could go down the animal's throat.

Fishing games: If you want to exercise your dog without constantly having to race along with it, and you can't find anyone to play with you, try using a fishing pole: Tie a toy to a short line at the end of a rod about 6.5 feet (2 m) long. Especially with young dogs, you can try out a variety of action games. Drag the object along the ground in a straight line or a zigzag. Lift it off the ground, dangle it in the air, jiggle it up and down, or move it in a circle. The purpose of these games is to stimulate controlled sequences of movements, and they are particularly important for puppies.

Use these games in combination with small hurdles to make your pet's first attempts at jumping easier.

A solo performance: Instead of the fishing pole, of course, you can set up a permanent place for your pet to play with a ball suspended from a rope or a knot in the end of the rope. Attach the rope to the frame of a child's swing set that is no longer in use, or to a tree limb, or something similar. The object should be suspended slightly above the dog's head, where the dog can jump at it to set it in motion (see HOW-TO: Games to Play in Your Yard, page 26).

Canine get-togethers. The yard offers excellent conditions for a play group made up of the neighborhood dogs. For puppies that have been immunized, this is great fun as well as a valuable means of training and socialization. Don't offer the lawn team the same toys that your pet plays with, because your dog will surely advance claims of ownership. Usually, the noisy group will be completely happy to play together, even without human inducement.

Your yard is part of your pet's territory; before adult dogs come over for a play session, you need to arrange a meeting on neutral ground where they can sniff each other first. Even with the most peaceable playmates, someone should supervise them at all times. When several dogs are playing enthusiastically, your commands and admonitions rarely have the desired effect. Protect your garden and flowerbeds with a portable fence before the rowdy bunch storms onto your lawn.

Important: Limit extensive yard training to a maximum of three 10-minute units a day. Basically, it is all right to play outdoors in any weather, except when the ground is frozen solid or when the midday heat is intense. After every feeding, wait at least one hour before letting your pet play. Please keep in mind that giant breeds such as Great Danes or Irish wolfhounds must not be allowed to play hard until the twelfth month of life, because their bone and muscles develop and mature later than in smaller breeds.

Some training is necessary before you can get the cheese to stay in place this way.

25

HOW-TO:
Games to Play in Your Yard

Ball Games
Drawing 1

When jumping, running in hot pursuit, or sprinting after a ball, the dog is training its motor sequences, reactions, and spatial visualization.

For rolling and throwing (as we discussed on page 24), small balls made of hard rubber are a good choice. With young dogs, vary the trend of play and the playing techniques. Roll the ball toward or away from the dog at different speeds, roll it out of the dog's field of vision, or over uneven ground to make it skip and hop to increase the dog's desire to get the ball under control. Combine such play with directing your dog to find and fetch objects. Start with easy curves thrown only a short distance but *never* directly at the dog!

Ball-boxing (see also page 24) with large lightweight or air-filled balls appeals to many dogs. This time you *can* throw the ball directly at the dog at medium height. The dog has to jump into the air at the right moment and propel the ball back in your direction, using its muzzle. In their passionate desire to hit the ball in the air, some dogs make a rather hard landing at times, so it is best to use this exercise on soft turf.

Don't leave air-filled balls with your dog when unsupervised, because they can be bitten and the pieces swallowed.

Driving the ball, running, and playing soccer, with the dog using its feet and sometimes its muzzle, are fun for a dog, even when playing alone; however, such play is more exciting when the animal's owner is an opponent. Never let your pet bite your shoes or clothing, even in the excitement of the game! Slow the pace by occasionally blocking the ball or interrupting play with the "Sit!" command.

1) Playing ball is an all-time favorite game.

Playing in a circle with two or three people is another exciting game. You can send the dog away in pursuit of the ball you have thrown to the other human players (see Drawing 1). At each position, allow the dog to take the ball briefly and play with it.

Note: You should never deliberately deceive a dog—that applies to all games in general. For instance, don't move your arm as if to throw a ball that you have concealed behind your back.

Educational Games
For puppies, playing means learning and gaining experience (see Puppies' World of Play, page 12).

Games of touch: Either make use of existing different types of surfaces in your yard such as grass, concrete, sand, or paving stones, or lay out special surfaces for your pet to touch. Wooden planks, plastic sheeting, aluminum foil, lengths of material, blankets, or a thick layer of fall leaves may be used. Toys or treats can be used to encourage a young dog to walk across the unaccustomed surfaces. If necessary, put the pup on its leash and accompany it. Give your pet plenty of time to sniff and test each new surface.

Curtain test: Fasten a dense curtain made of aluminum strips or plastic ribbons to metal supports or a wooden frame. Place it so that the dog cannot go around it. From the other side of the curtain, call your dog by name and say "Come!" If the puppy balks repeatedly, lead it on leash up to the curtain, push the strips aside with one hand, and gently tug on the leash to get the dog to walk through, holding out a treat, if necessary.

Solo Games
Drawing 2

Solo play does not mean playing unsupervised in the yard! The owner determines the time and duration of play and keeps an eye on the "soloist" at all times.

Training Your Pet to Do Tricks

Practicing and mastering little tricks and stunts is something that almost all dogs enjoy. This activity exercises the brain more than the body. When the dog succeeds, its owner is proud, and the animal enjoys receiving praise and being the center of attention.

Catching treats in the air: In the preliminary training, hold a treat above the dog's head. When you say "Stay!" it should not react, but when you say "Hup!" it should snatch the food. Then teach it the trick. With one hand, hold its muzzle shut from below and keep its head still. Place a cube of cheese or a small dog treat on the top of its muzzle. During the learning phase, hold its head firmly while repeating the "Stay!" command. Each time you repeat the trick, relax your hand a bit, until it is no longer touching the dog. Say "Hup!" to direct it to toss the cube into the air with its muzzle and catch it in its open mouth. Do not let your pet pick up bites

2) Playing alone with a ball fastened to a rope.

that have fallen to the ground (see photos, pages 24 and 25).

Note: This trick is not suitable for breeds with a short muzzle.

Rolling over: This is a trick that many dogs love to perform. After you say "Down!" use your hands to roll the dog over to one side, while you give an appropriate command ("Roll!"). Reward your pet, and repeat.

Other Games for the Yard
Drawing 3

Tug-of-war: Use only sturdy material, such as jute sewed together in several layers to resist tear. Ropes should not be spliced or made of sharp-edged plastic fibers. One requirement: the dog has to obey the command "Out!" This exercise is not advised for dominant males and aggressive dogs.

Hiding, seeking, and retrieving games where a scent is laid: The yard offers interesting, challenging variations on the game of hide-and-seek. Possible hiding places are found everywhere, including under leaves, in barrels, suspended from branches, and many others. This game involves laying down a scent trail with treats, a sweater belonging to the dog's owner, a favorite toy, or a blanket that the dog snuggles with. This exercise is one way to set complicated tasks for dogs with experienced noses.

Digging box: Your dog's own private sandbox will give it a chance to engage in its beloved digging activity without fear of punishment. To ensure that it digs in its box and nowhere else, regularly direct it to find toys that you have hidden in the sand (see Drawing 3). That will strengthen the tie with the sandbox and help to keep your pet away from cultivated plants.

3) A sandbox of its own to dig in is paradise for a dog. It can root around there to its heart's content, without being punished.

An Obstacle Course in the Yard

With imagination and a little know-how, you can quickly and inexpensively build all the obstacles yourself (see page 30).

• Plan a course that can be left in place for months during good weather. Choose construction materials that are portable and easily stored.

• Use only materials on which your dog cannot injure itself. Use nontoxic and environmentally friendly paints and varnishes on wood.

• Tables and planks should be sufficiently stable, and should stand level on a firm surface, so that they will not tip over.

• The hurdle tops (bricks, bars) should not be fastened to the obstacles, but supported so as to yield or be dislodged upon contact. Insert the slalom poles in special, flexible rubber cuffs, or set them only a few inches deep into soft ground.

• The surface of the course should not be made of materials, such as clay, that become soft or slippery when wet.

The Obstacle Course: What Really Matters

The most suitable obstacles are tires, tunnels, inclined planks, slalom poles, broad jumps, and high jumps (see page 54).

Hurdles: A dog hardly needs motivational aids to train it to jump. On the contrary, its enthusiasm usually has to be restrained and limits imposed on training times. Reward it only when it jumps specified hurdles on the course, and do not encourage your pet to jump over every available obstacle in the yard, such as hedges, benches, ponds, or raised planting areas.

Fixed obstacles always present a risk of injury, and areas used for takeoffs and landings might be in parts of the yard that are off-limits to your pet (see Taboo Areas, page 22).

In the learning process, high jumps should precede jumping through a tire—which requires considerable effort and far more body control.

Tunnels: Never start with a long, dark tunnel that might frighten or discourage your dog. Make a short, bright tunnel (out of light-colored fabric, for example). In addition, the dog should see a familiar face at the other end of the tunnel. During the initial training, a tentlike structure made from a tarpaulin or blanket is adequate. The height of the tunnel depends on the size of the dog's body.

Cross-over: Building a tunnel yourself is less costly than constructing an inclined wall that meets specifications of Agility trials.

Slalom poles: Begin with only five poles, and leave broad intervals between them. The short course allows the handler ample opportunity to make the rules of the task clear to the dog. The poles need to bend when touched by the dog (to set up slalom poles, see page 31).

To Make the Obstacle Course Training Easier

• Before training on an obstacle course, teach your dog the basic commands.

• Trust and a close bond with the dog handler are important prerequisites for the animal's motivation and cooperation.

• During training, encourage your dog with a toy or a bit of food; for example, toss the toy or treat across the hurdle. As your pet negotiates the obstacle course, accompany it with audible signals, such as "Over!" Body language is

A dog traversing an obstacle course is under stress because it wants to do its best for its owner. After it has succeeded, always praise your pet. You might also play with it or go for a short walk with your pet to help it work off its excitement.

For young dogs, paw contact with a variety of different surfaces is an important experience.

also important. An outstretched palm is a signal to stop. Treats and toys should not be needed here; the goal is for the dog to demonstrate its willingness to perform an assignment for its owner without rewards other than praise.
• If your pet loses its motivation, find out the causes. Perhaps you have over-done it with strenuous training. Health problems and boredom also interfere with motivation. If necessary, take a break from the training for a while, or select a simpler, shorter obstacle course.

Note: With all obstacle courses, the object is correct performance on the part of the dog.

HOW-TO:
Building an Obstacle Course for Your Yard

Tips for Do-It-Yourself Obstacles

Wood is the building material of choice. It is easy to work with, and no special tools are needed. With proper treatment, it will withstand wind and weather, and it is sufficiently sturdy. Always use finished lumber, preferably with smooth, rounded edges. As mentioned on page 20, when weatherproofing and painting, make sure to use non-toxic, environmentally safe solutions and paints. Galvanized bolts, nails, bars, and washers should be used, and sharp ends must be countersunk in surfaces used for running and jumping.

High Jump
<u>Drawing 1</u>

A good choice for the cross-piece is a broomstick or a plastic bar. Lay the bar loosely on pedestals of adjustable height; if possible use three-legged supports, pieces of log, special high-jump columns, or stools. To keep the dog from running around the side of the obstacle, or slipping underneath the bar, put up cloths or blankets as visual shields.

Learning phase: Initially, the height of the crosspiece should be just above ground level at about 8 inches (20 cm). Encourage the dog, on leash, with a slight tug accompanied by the "Over!" command.

Tire Jump

For this exercise, select a car tire with not too small an inner diameter. For larger dogs, use truck or tractor tires. Suspend the tire from a tree branch, securing it at the bottom and top with two ropes or chains on each side, so the tire cannot turn and twist; or suspend it in a rectangular frame. Fill the lower inside part of the tire with sand or dirt to prevent the dog's legs from getting caught when it jumps.

Learning phase: When the training starts, have the lower part of the tire resting on the ground; then gradually raise it as training progresses.

Tunnel
<u>Drawing 2</u>

You can build a tunnel with U-shaped devices or poles tied together at acute angles, like tent poles, with the grass as the base. The internal height depends on the height of your dog. Do not force it to crawl through the tunnel. Cover the framework with plastic sheeting or tarps.

1) The height of the crossbar for the high jump needs to be very low at first.

Learning phase: Start with a tunnel section about 3 feet (1 m) long, and coax the dog through from the opposite end. Gradually lengthen the tunnel, so that ultimately your pet will go through long, dark sections. Later, you can include curves and angles in the tunnel.

Inclined Wall

The wall (A-frame) is composed of two identical ramps constructed of lengths of plywood. In regulated competition, they are required to meet at an angle of 90 degrees, with the highest point about 76 inches (193 cm) off the ground. In your yard, you can use a smaller-scale arrangement. During the learning phase, I recommend that you construct the wall so that the ramps are close to ground level, with a very slight slope. On the walking surface, attach slats 2 to 4 inches (5–10 cm) wide and 10 inches (25 cm) apart to keep the dog from slipping. To prevent injuries, cover the ridge at the top with a guard strip made of rubber.

Learning phase: The inclined wall is a contact obstacle, not a hurdle! Put your pet on leash to familiarize it with the wall by walking slowly across it. Have a second person walk at the dog's other side to prevent it from jumping off or turning around prematurely (see Important for Agility Athletes, page 31).

2) With blankets and U-shaped devices or poles, you can easily build a tunnel in your yard so that the future Agility athlete can acquire early experience.

under a board, get the dog used to a surface that moves. The diameter of the pole will determine the intensity of the seesaw effect.

Learning phase: Slowly lead your pet, on leash, past the point where the board begins to tilt—up one side and down the other.

Important: To prevent injuries in an obstacle race, the dog should not wear a collar. I recommend all-in-one leashes for training your dog because they are quickly and easily removed.

Note: Keep your dog's nails trimmed closely to keep them from getting caught on obstacles.

Important for Agility Athletes

If you would like to participate in Agility competition with your dog (see page 54), you should train under conditions approximating those specified in the official Agility rules, even in the improvised obstacle course in your yard.

Slalom Poles

Drawing 3

To complete this obstacle course, a course marked by poles should be negotiated, alternating from right to left. The five poles should be driven into soft ground or inserted into special rubber sleeves so they will bend when touched. Good choices for poles are round pieces of wood, broomsticks, or thin, light plastic tubes.

Learning phase: During this phase, set up a few poles in a straight line at wide intervals, about the length of the dog's body. Lead your dog through the course, keeping its leash perpendicular to the ground. Changes in direction are signaled by a tug on the leash or by knee pressure, and perhaps holding out a treat as an inducement. The slalom poles require a high level of concentration and cooperation on the dogs' part. Dogs would naturally prefer to negotiate this

section of the obstacle course in a straight line. If your dog repeatedly tries to take shortcuts after the learning phase is over, start practicing with your pet on leash again.

Seesaw

Drawing 4

Building a workable seesaw is costly. Here's a tried and true alternative: With a pole placed

3) When your pet is learning, set the slalom poles far apart.

4) A round log and a board will make a simple seesaw.

Games for the Great Outdoors

A Great Adventure: Physical Fitness

Exploration of nearby areas outside your yard can provide diversion for both playing and training. After a few weeks in a yard, your dog will have every square foot committed to memory, and the usual routes taken to sniffing and toilet areas become boring. Familiar habitats are taken for granted and the other side of the fence becomes more inviting. Pets appreciate new vistas and enjoy the excitement of discovery.

Before taking a trip outside your pet's usual boundaries, you should plan a program of new games and training exercises to add to the joy of the trips. Usual obstacles, toys, and sports equipment can be left at home. New environments call for improvisation, using materials at hand. Suitable places for outdoor sports and games abound, and play activities are limited only by your imagination.

Limits on Playing Outdoors

• In the woods, every dog should be kept on leash; frequently, however, dog owners mistakenly ignore this requirement. Only if your dog obeys perfectly should it be allowed off leash, but it must be kept under verbal control, and within your field of vision. Even with the best training, dogs with a pronounced hunting instinct often cannot be stopped once they have picked up a scent. Such dogs must always be on leash in the woods.

• Never let the dog run into the underbrush and bushes; let it play only on paths or at the edges of paths.
• In spring and fall, be especially mindful of the young of wild animals and ground-nesting birds, particularly at the edges of forested land and in meadows.
• During the winter (especially in snow), wild animals are affected by any kind of disturbance. In trying to flee from a pursuing dog, they lose a great deal of strength.
• All directional signs should be heeded and all regulations obeyed.
• In natural ponds and in places where swimming birds raise their young, dogs should not be permitted to swim.
• Many seaside resorts do not allow dogs to be taken to the main beach; often, however, certain portions of beach where dogs are allowed are marked with signs.
• Avoid loud commands and continued barking in woods and fields. Conscientious dog owners respect natural quiet and peaceful surroundings.

Exploring Together

In your yard you can plan all types of games and sports, but when out hiking or walking, you need to be on the lookout for suitable places to play. Dogs love the status quo in many respects. That certainly applies to the hierarchy within the family, the rules of the household, and their food. Outdoors, however, they are grateful for every exciting, exotic scent.

Digging is great fun for most dogs but they need to learn where digging is allowed and where it is prohibited.

For the initial balancing exercises, use a large log.

Vary the routes you use for walking your dog as much as possible. Incorporate little side trips, switch to a route that runs parallel to your usual route, or set out in a direction other than your customary one. You can also put your dog into the car, drive for ten minutes, and find a new wonderland of smells to put under its nose.

Places to Play Outdoors

Set out with your pet to search jointly for the playgrounds of your dreams.

Fallen logs are ideal for training your dog to jump and for balancing. First, practice jumping over small logs and balancing on large ones. Use only logs lying near the path; never venture far from the forest paths.

Layers of leaves and loose soil are good for hiding a variety of objects such as toys or treats brought from home. The intense, strange smells and the chance to dig unreprimanded appeal to your dog's scent and discovery talents.

Trees, barns, sheds, banks of earth act as barriers to screen you from view when playing hide-and-seek. As a rule, play such games only if you have a second person along to hold the dog still until you give the "Seek" command.

Different types of soil structures, including leaves and high grass, can be used to lay out scents for tracking.

Large open areas such as flat expanses of grass and lawn, or remote places where there is no traffic, are ideal playgrounds. City parks with wide paths and possibly beaches provide other diversions. For playing without having to keep the dog near you, try ball games, Frisbee tossing, and other games involving fetching and running.

Small open areas along paths in woods, fields, edges of meadows, and beaches lend themselves to games that involve physical proximity such as catch, dexterity exercises, tug-of-war, and tussling games.

Rounded peaks and hills often provide low, natural obstacles to jump over. They are fine for training your pet to run and sprint and for improving overall fitness.

Asphalt paths in woods and fields can be used for jogging or for running alongside your bike.

Water in lakes, streams, or rivers invite swimming, possibly in combination with retrieving.

Important: Always avoid playing on children's playgrounds, on adventure playgrounds, on busy streets, and in public parking areas. Stay in pet-designated areas of city parks and communal greenbelts. Don't play in pedestrian zones, away from paths in wooded areas, or in fields. To protect wildlife, avoid underbrush, and hedges especially during nesting season. Follow signs when in nature or wildlife conservation areas, and near ponds and lakes. Stay away from areas where there is rabies or a threat of rabies, as designated by signs or notices. Open-air restaurants are off-limits as well as someone else's private property, including

Playing alone is fun, but it is always much better when there are two.

Games for a Crowd

When a large number of other dogs are involved, playing becomes a wonderful experience for your pet. Whether it takes place during a group walk in the morning or in a meadow, conflict and friction are rare, and the enjoyment is enormous.

• A prerequisite for harmonious play is that all the dogs are off leash.

• Overly zealous players should be taken out of the group temporarily and calmed down. In general, go with the group dynamics. Minor disagreements almost always resolve themselves. If owners try to act as peacemakers, however, jealous scenes are not uncommon.

• Don't allow toys into play that might precipitate quarreling over whose possessions they are.

• Allow the group to decide what and how to play. In addition to games of chase and races, combative games and rooting and digging in the ground together are especially popular. Over time, small groups are often formed by dogs that develop closer friendships.

• If a new dog joins the group, it should be allowed to enter into contact unhindered. Only boisterous members of the group need to be leashed during the early, introductory sniffing phase.

• For puppies, play groups have a valuable socializing effect. My recommendations are to enroll your young dog early in a special puppy school, if one is available.

• Before beginning group play, keep in mind that it is difficult to intervene once group play has begun—you have decidedly less influence than when playing with your pet one-on-one.

driveways, front yards, and parking zones, even if they are not fenced.

Important Aspects of Outdoor Play

Playing time: During hot summer months, move your games and sports to the cooler morning and evening hours and limit physical activity in general.

Tick protection: At the peak of the tick season (early summer to fall), try to avoid tall grass and shrubs as much as possible. After every walk, inspect the dog for parasites, and be sure it wears a tick collar. There is risk from tick bites for both dogs and humans.

Leash requirement: In hunting zones of woods and fields near woods, dogs with a strong drive to hunt and chase game have to be on leash at all times. With an extra-long leash (about 33 feet [10 m]), playing will still be fun.

Terrain inspection: Before you allow your pet to play in unfamiliar terrain or to jump into a lake or pond, check the ground for dangers such as metal, glass, sharp rocks, and holes. Inspect the shore and wading zone for foreign objects and sharp-edged seashells.

Visual contact: Especially in the woods, a dog should never be out of verbal control distance. It should never be out of sight or more than about 33 feet (10 m) away from its owner. Only then can you react and call to your pet if it suddenly scents game. In addition, you will avoid confrontations with the forest rangers who may ask you to leave the woods.

Games Are Not Always Power Play

Outdoor games need not always be synonymous with competitive athletics and power play. Try little games and limited play sessions:

Be careful when playing on a hard surface.

• They are especially beneficial for young dogs acquiring their first experiences of the great outdoors when they are introduced to new terrain, obstacles, scents, and noises.

• "Body school" lessons are games to improve the young dog's motor coordination. They can be started in your home and yard and continued as little outdoor activities.

• Little games are just right for dogs with diminished capability including elderly, sick, convalescent, or pregnant dogs. They serve as motivations for dogs that are reluctant participants in other activities.

• Action games have to be canceled in very hot weather because of the risk of heatstroke or heart and circulatory problems. In extremely cold weather, there is risk of injury on frozen ground. Only limited play should be allowed in heavy rain. These are times for little outdoor games and indoor games.

• Dogs that are kept on leash because of their tendency to fight, stray, or hunt can still have a chance for fun and exercise playing games while on long leashes.

What Can You and Your Dog Play Outdoors?

Games of agility: These are games such as balancing on logs. At least with inexperienced dogs, check the logs before the first session to see that they are positioned to avoid danger of slipping or tilting. Check their condition, by looking for cracks, crevices, and protruding branches. Loose bark, slippery patches of lichen and moss, or rotten wood can create hazards to inexperienced dogs. Choose only logs near a path, never off in the woods. Naturally, outdoors you also can practice dexterity tests from the repertoire of tricks previously described, including teaching your

• Even if very little time is available, you usually can fit in a quick game as a welcome break.

• Sometimes only a small amount of time is available, such as 15-minute rest breaks during a vacation trip. Little outdoor games require no advance planning, few resources, and only a small amount of room.

• Usually your dog stays fairly close to you during little games. These are important to strengthen a dog's trust in its owner and reinforce the bond between owner and pet.

pet to roll over, sit up on its hind legs, and offer a paw.

Games involving seeking and fetching: Playing these games outdoors means playing at the third level of difficulty. Usually you will have begun puppy training with easy tasks indoors, followed by hide-and-seek games in the yard, which require considerably more experience on the dog's part. Finally, outdoors, away from home, the games reach the expert level. They involve new surroundings, unfamiliar hiding places in what frequently is difficult terrain. There are more distractions due to unfamiliar smells, sounds, passersby, and other dogs. Never ask your dog to do the impossible, and always give it support ("Seek here!") if it is confused. To maintain its interest in playing seeking games, it needs to be able to find every hiding place. Hiding places in leaves and loose dirt encourage the dog to dig and increase its enjoyment of the game. For the dog with a good nose, combine seeking games with the laying of scents using treats, rawhide bones, or clothing.

Hiding: Games of hide-and-seek are an ideal way to strengthen the relationship between owner and pet, providing education without obedience drills. As with seeking and fetching, basic obedience training is a prerequisite to playing hide-and-seek. In these games, the dog is off leash. It has to obey the basic commands "Sit!" "Down!" "Come!" and "Out!"

Tussling, tug-of-war, and tag: The typical indoor and yard games can also be played out in open country whenever it is necessary to keep dogs on leash for play. The leash is obligatory when near traffic routes, when making a rest stop on trips, or in areas where rabies is a threat. Leashes should also be used in unfamiliar terrain, in areas where there are game animals or game

Jogging together strengthens the bond between dog and owner.

preserves, and with dogs that stray, fight, are in heat, or possess an exceedingly strong hunting instinct. The radius of play can be extended with a long leash that is available in pet stores.

Toys: A bite ring, favorite toy, small wooden dumbbell, or rubber ball may be taken along to allow you to play with your dog on leash at close range. Many dogs enjoy carrying some of their toys, especially a ball or wooden dumbbell, during the walk.

HOW-TO:
Games with That Certain Something

Seeking and Fetching
Drawing 1

These games are suitable only for dogs that have completed their basic training. It is particularly important that your pet obey the commands "Come!" and "Out!"

As in your home and yard, begin with simple seeking tasks, with the object clearly visible or right next to the path. Later on, increase the level of difficulty by hiding it in tall grass, behind trees, under leaves, and in loose soil.

If necessary, practice with your pet on a long leash, to lend emphasis to the retrieve commands ("Come!" and "Fetch!"). After the dog has found the hidden object and picked it up, tug the leash gently while you give the command. Allowing your pet to dig for objects hidden in leaves or loose soil is a powerful motivation for games of this type.

Difficult hiding places, including those in which the object is covered over, buried, or far away, should be combined with laying a trail. Trail scent marks of favorite toys, wooden dumbbells, rawhide bones, treats, or pieces of old clothing work well. In all games involving seeking and fetching, it is helpful to have a second person to restrain the dog until you give the "Seek!" command. These games foster a dog's individual initiative and tracking abil-

ity, as well as its overall training and obedience.

Balancing
Drawing 2

The balancing exercise is a standard game for cross-country runners. Before the initial lessons, test the log's suitability (see What Can You and Your Dog Play Outdoors?, page 36). Choose a log with a large diameter. Run beside your leashed dog and, if necessary, give it some support while it balances on the log. Let the dog set the pace. As your pet becomes more adept, try the game, without the leash, staying close to your dog at first.

Once it has mastered the technique, almost every dog will balance eagerly and voluntarily, and with increasing self-confidence will begin to search out logs of its own accord. As a rule, no special commands are necessary, although a verbal "Hup!" to encourage it to jump onto the log may be needed. Let your pet balance only where a soft surface will cushion a possible fall. Never

1) It is harder to play "seek" games outdoors than indoors.

2) First teach your pet to balance on a big log.

allow it to run on walls or railings above concrete or stone surfaces.

Hiding
Drawing 3

When you want to hide and let your pet find you, the help of a human companion is absolutely essential. The other person can supervise the dog or divert its attention until you have found a place to hide.

In the basic exercise, the dog watches as the human goes toward a hiding place behind a tree or around a barn, shed, rock, or wall. Once the person to be found is out of sight, the dog is called into action with the "Seek!" command. At the same time, the dog's handler, from his or her hiding place, calls the dog's name.

Important: Praise your pet enthusiastically as soon as it has found you.

In advanced training, the dog is no longer allowed to watch while you hide, but you still call its name from your hiding place. Later, only the "Seek!" command is given and more difficult hiding places are chosen. As the dog's competence improves, you can hide on a lower limb of a tree, in a barn, behind large obstacles, or on the other side of ditches or creeks.

Things to Take Along

For short play breaks during a walk, it generally is best to choose small, lightweight playthings, such as bite rings, solid rubber balls, lightweight wooden dumbbells, squeak toys, and other favorite items. The objects you select will determine the kind of game you play—throwing and catching games with the ball, tussling and playing tug-of-war with the ring or a rope, playing fetch with the wooden dumbbell or squeak toys (see drawings, pages 14 and 15).

Games with toys that you take along offer certain advantages and are recommended for dogs on leash as well. Very little space is

3) To play hide-and-seek with your pet, you need two people.

required, so these games can be played almost everywhere, for example, with your pet on leash during rest stops on a car trip. Spontaneous games foster close ties between owner and pet and promote alertness. They can be used purposefully to distract your pet, for example, when near wild game or canine rivals, and to reduce nervousness and excitement.

4) Being asked to carry something, such as a small stick, fills a dog with pride. Performing such jobs keeps leash-biters from gnawing at the leash.

Carrying Tasks

Drawing 4

Actually, these are not games in the narrower sense of the word, yet for many dogs they provide the greatest pleasure to be experienced between their own front door and the path in the woods. Proudly, carefully, and with great devotion, dogs love to perform little transportation tasks set by their owner. Appropriate objects include lightweight wooden dumbbells, short, smooth sticks, and certain toys and balls.

Caution: It is dangerous for your dog to carry tree limbs and

branches! A dog is unable to estimate the width of the object it carries in its mouth, and may experience collisions with pedestrians or cyclists that can cause injuries to dog and human.

Other Do's and Don'ts

• Avoid games on surfaces that are painful to dogs' feet or those that may cause injuries. Stay off

crushed-rock paths, asphalt that has been softened by the sun, or frozen paths and sidewalks strewn with thawing salt.

• When away from home, in unfamiliar surroundings, always play with your dog on leash at first.

• Pet-sitters should be instructed not to play any close-contact games such as tussling or tug-of-war with your pet. Toys used in such play should be stored out of reach of your dog during your absence.

• Take a break after every meal (with large dogs, rest for at least two hours).

The two dogs wait eagerly to see what toy their owner has to offer. When several dogs play together, they usually come up with their own ideas for games as well.

Going All Out in Games and Sports

Restrained, gentle play is just as much fun as concentrated play that takes mental effort. Nonetheless, all healthy dogs need an opportunity to play in an unrestrained manner on a regular basis.

• A dog is born to run and to move about extensively. When it engages in both short-term and repetitive activities, it has a chance to test its aptitudes and needs for action.

• Enjoyment of play and physical activity are important yardsticks for measuring the state of your pet's health. In active play, an owner can detect possible lamenesses or injuries to the locomotor system.

• Action games not involving physical closeness promote obedience in your pet.

• Complaining or nervous dogs are generally much more affable and even-tempered after physical exertion.

• Success and the ability to master a task, such as during a swimming session or a game of Frisbee, will promote the dog's cooperation and improve its personality.

• Action games improve motor skills and coordination of movement, especially in young dogs.

• Physical exercises, if prescribed appropriately and purposefully, speed physical and emotional healing processes. They are also indispensable, along with diet control, for helping overweight dogs shed their excess poundage.

Playgrounds for "Athletes"

All-out activities should not be timed with a stopwatch, and you should let your dog engage in such play only in places where it can go all out without hindrance or danger. Even for games and sports in the great outdoors, there are limits and prohibitions on play. With all-out games, even more than with little games, the quality of the play area is very important: It must be free of waste and trash, especially glass, cans, and discarded plastic. It should also be free of holes and ditches, some of which may be concealed under leaves or tall grass. Play areas should be confined to ground that is not extremely steep or slippery. Where streets, houses, walls, or fences border the terrain, organize the game toward the center of the play area. Before jumping over natural obstacles, such as logs or creeks, make sure the landing zone is safe.

Athletic running activities such as Frisbee and ball games require large open spaces or areas with little foot traffic. Running games are best pursued in broad treeless meadows, on wide forest and field paths, in field boundaries, or along the edges of woods. In cities, open space is sometimes found in empty parks or on

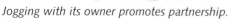

Jogging with its owner promotes partnership.

school playgrounds on weekends. Be sure to obtain permission before exercising your dog in any public facility, and always look for signs that restrict pet activities.

Important Tips on Training

• When trotting along next to a bicycle or jogging with its owner, a dog should be kept on the curbside or toward the edge of the path. Being off leash is a privilege reserved exclusively for dogs that can be relied upon to heel. Only dogs that always come back to the shore on command can be allowed to swim in a lake without being on leash.

• Dogs with a pronounced hunting instinct cannot be allowed off leash in areas where game abounds. Use leashes on dogs that want to chase joggers, cyclists, cats, and squirrels. To discourage a leashed dog from chasing, give its collar a sharp jerk at the first sign of its intention to give pursuit. At the same time, say "Bad dog!" or "No!" Never scold your pet when it returns from chasing something; it relates the reprimand to its return.

• Rolling in feces, picking up dead small animals, and eating excrement may not seriously harm a dog, but it will spoil the game for its human playmate! To discourage the habit, lay out suitable bait, but pull your dog's leash, saying "Bad dog!" or "No!" just before it picks up the object. Repeat the lesson until it leaves the object alone solely on command, without your tugging the leash. Reward every successful performance.

• When playing with young dogs, always make allowances for the fact that they tire more easily and have less physical strength. Large breed puppies in particular, whose bodies take longer to develop than those of small breeds,

should not be subjected to significant stress before they are one year old.

• On rainy days or when there is deep snow, limit action games with your pet. Omit such play altogether in extremely cold weather when the ground is icy or frozen.

• Giant breeds and large, heavy dogs should not be allowed to play outdoors during the heat of summer. The same applies for dogs that are overweight, or very old.

• Be sure to supervise children when playing with all dogs.

• Always conclude the training session while the dog is still participating enthusiastically. Once it loses interest or overexerts itself, future play sessions will be less appreciated by the pet.

Please Show Consideration

It is not often that you and your pet will have a sufficiently large area for games and sports all to yourselves— whether in parks, wooded areas belonging to the city, or other nearby recreational areas. Please remember that a dog that is running loose can arouse fear in walkers, joggers, cyclists, and children. Even if you know that your pet is extremely gentle, you need to be able to summon it to you promptly and call a halt to the game.

Many children and some adults are frightened of *all* dogs, regardless of the circumstances. Friendly, tail-wagging puppies with excellent intentions may be as frightening as aggressive, bad-tempered dogs. Any dog of any size or age may cause fear reactions in some people. When approached by a dog, frightened people may react by screaming, kicking at the dog, waving their arms, or running away. Any of those panicky actions may trigger defensive posturing by the dog—it may snap, snarl, or begin chasing them.

Never forget to put some edible rewards, such as dry food or snack sticks, in your pocket before setting out for the playground.

Many dogs, like this retriever, are enthusiastic swimmers.

Great Games for Going All Out

For instructions on teaching your dog the games described below, see HOW-TO: Going All Out, page 46.

Ball games: Ideally, you will find an area the size of a soccer field, for your dog that is a sports enthusiast. With a wide open field and a good throwing arm, you will both enjoy lively, unrestrained ball games. Long-range throws of a solid rubber ball will train your pet's reactions, sprinting ability, and endurance. During such play, your pet has to obey when you direct it to come or fetch. Large balls inflated with air are good for games of fetch, with the dog driving the ball. Ball-boxing, where the ball is returned with a thrust of the muzzle, is a great sport. Soccer games in which owner and pet try to steal the ball from each other are also more fun on a wide playing field.

Frisbee: Many dogs develop incredible skill at catching the disk-shaped plastic toy. Use only undamaged disks, with no cracks, broken places, or sharp plastic edges. Give preference to lightweight Frisbees, if possible with soft rims. Practice your throwing technique without your pet at first, to perfect your throwing skill and accuracy.

Jumping: Gradually, your dog will learn its jumping capacity by experimenting with logs of different sizes. At first, give it support, and practice with relatively small-diameter logs and with your pet on leash.

Swimming: Never drag or throw your pet into the water! Practice the dog's retrieval exercises in an area near the shore, and "accidentally" throw a familiar object into shallow water. If necessary, go into the lake or river with your dog. Avoid whirlpools, strong currents, and water with undercurrents that may be barely visible at the surface. Dogs shake themselves vigorously when they come out of the water so make sure that no uninvolved bystander gets sprayed with water. Some breeds have little talent for swimming. They include bulldogs, basset hounds, and dachshunds (their bodies are not built for it). Some dogs enjoy boating with their owner, and a few will ride on a surfboard when windsurfing in a light breeze and close to shore. Others love races and games of ball or Frisbee on a sandy beach. Make sure that your pet is not exposed to blazing sunlight for too long without frequent stops in a shady spot.

Jogging: This is a good activity for dogs and humans who are in condition. Keep the dog on leash, with the leash slightly slack, while the dog runs beside you. Start with relatively short distances (1.2 mile, [2 km] at most), and increase the distance slowly. Jog long distances (over 3 miles [5 km]) only with well-conditioned dogs that are tireless athletes, such as greyhounds, Irish setters, hunting dogs, and herding dogs. Select paths with surfaces that are as yielding as possible. Don't jog with your pet in hot weather or in snow and ice.

Sight hounds, such as whippets and greyhounds may enjoy training regularly at a racetrack. These breeds are track hounds, and should never be allowed to run loose in open areas! An alternative to racing is coursing, where the dogs run in pursuit of an artificial hare, pulled along the ground in a zigzag path.

Bicycling: Try this only after preliminary training, and only with steady dogs that lack hunting instinct and will run alongside the bike at an even pace. Never tie the leash to the bicycle frame. If necessary, use aids such as special spring-loaded leash holders with springs that are attached at rear wheel level (available in bicycle shops and pet stores).

Caution: Tree limbs and large branches are not suitable objects for throwing. If a dog snaps at a sharp-pointed, awkwardly shaped limb that is about to hit the ground, serious injuries to your pet's head, mouth, and throat can result. Also, training your pet to race alongside a moving car is *not* part of an acceptable sports program. If you are out for more than an hour, make sure your dog has access to cool clean drinking water.

First Aid for Injuries

No dog is invulnerable—your pet can hurt itself, collapse from exhaustion or heatstroke, or consume poisonous substances.

Bites or Lacerations

For heavily bleeding bites or lacerations resulting from dog fights, sharp branches, or pieces of glass, apply a pressure bandage over the wound, if possible. If you have no gauze bandage with a compress on hand, cover the wound with a clean handkerchief and wrap a stocking or a scarf around it. Do not leave the pressure bandage in place longer than an hour. Open wounds and punctures should be treated by a veterinarian immediately.

Heatstroke

If you suspect heatstroke, carry the dog into the shade, and use cold water to carefully cool its feet, legs, and body. Never lay its entire body in the water! Symptoms of heatstroke are heavy drooling, uncoordinated movements, staggering or tottering. Heatstroke can be fatal, and exercise in extremely hot weather or blazing sun should be avoided.

Important: If you suspect that your dog has been injured, get it to the veterinarian without delay.

If a dog is in great pain or if an accident has confused it or caused it to panic, it may bite—even its beloved owner. If necessary, tie a cloth (stocking, scarf) around its muzzle, and take it to a veterinarian immediately.

HOW-TO:
Going All Out

Ball Games

Retrieving balls presupposes obedience. That is important to ensure that all concerned have fun playing in an "orderly" way, without having to continually search for the dog or the ball. Obedient response to commands also helps to rule out potential dangers. For example, while searching for the ball the dog may suddenly catch the fresh scent of a rabbit, or people out for a stroll or strange dogs may cross its path. Your dog must be trained to respond immediately when you give the "Come!" or "Here!" commands. I recommend obedience training with a special dog whistle, so that your pet will respond to a whistled signal. Dog whistles produce very high-pitched tones, scarcely perceptible to humans, though dogs hear them even at a great distance.

Long-range tosses: These inspire enthusiasm in every dog. Your pet can run long distances, which is good training for its reactions, sprinting ability, and endurance. Searching for the ball, which often will have landed out of sight, trains its nose to follow a scent.

"Soccer" and other ball games: When playing "soccer" together, owner and pet try to steal the ball from one another. This sport may stimulate aggression in the dog if it tries to establish dominance. If the dog becomes aggressive, end the game!

Large, air-filled balls, such as those used to play soccer, are also good for playing fetch. Kick the ball away, and send the dog after it by saying "Fetch!" or "Bring!" By pushing the ball with its muzzle and hitting it with its paws, the dog will drive the ball back to you. Some dogs can even negotiate slalom poles in an obstacle course while pushing the ball with their muzzles.

Always keep your dog under verbal control when off leash.

Swimming
<u>Drawing 1</u>

First, introduce your dog to water in a shallow wading pool in your yard. Then let the puppy splash and play in the shallow water close to shore. With a small ball or toy that will float, slowly coax the dog to come farther into the water. Or, practice fetching on the shore, close to the water, and "accidentally" throw the ball into the lake or creek, after testing the speed of the current. With dogs that are apprehensive or afraid of water, set a good example by going into the water first, then encouraging

them to follow. The first time they feel the ground disappear under their feet, some dogs react by paddling rather frantically, but they usually realize quickly that there is no need to panic. When playing in open water, don't let the dog get too close to you in order to avoid painful scratches from contact with its nails. Swimming is an exercise that places little stress on joints, making it the ideal sport for all dogs with bone problems and for young dogs whose skeletal system is not yet fully developed.

Important: Never forcibly drag the dog into the water or throw it into the water.

Playing Frisbee

When you buy a Frisbee, look for a small, lightweight type, and make sure it has rounded edges or a rim area made of a soft material. Frisbees should not flutter, wobble, or suddenly drop to the ground. Stable paths of flight prevent injuries to your dog. Never throw the disk straight at your pet, but always at a sharp angle. Try to produce gradual angles of climb—then the Frisbee

1) Some dogs are afraid of the water at first. But when the ball "inadvertently" lands in shallow water during a game of fetch, the first steps will be easier to take.

will sink gently to the ground and will not plunge toward the dog from a great height. Playing Frisbee is exhausting; therefore, the intensity and length of play should be limited for older and overweight dogs. It is not a suitable activity for dogs with chronic skeletal problems, such as hip dysplasia.

Important: Cracked or broken Frisbees are dangerous and should be discarded.

Jumping
Drawing 2

Let your pet practice jumping with little logs that have a small diameter. With the dog on leash, climb over the log, keeping the leash slack, and encourage the dog to follow. Use the command "Hup!" or "Over!" and call the dog by name. Use words, suggestive gestures, and a treat or a toy if necessary to coax it to follow. After every successful attempt, praise the dog or give it a treat. Slowly increase the height of the obstacles. As soon as the dog's confidence and technique are where you want them to be, practice without the leash.

Jogging
The right introduction is important for moving at a constant pace. The dog should first master the command "Heel!" at a walking pace, staying on leash at your side. Then speed up the pace from a walk to a slow trot. The actual distance you cover is less important than the dog's ability to keep the leash slack and to stay parallel with you, without making stops to sniff along the way. While you jog, give the dog praise and encouragement. If it tries to run too fast or comes to a sudden halt, remotivate it by tugging at the leash and saying "Heel!" Limit the distance you cover in hot weather and on hard ground such as concrete or asphalt. Young dogs have limited ability to jog long distances and reach full capability only after a year old.

Running Next to a Bicycle
Drawing 3

Special training is even more important for your dog when learning to run beside a bicycle. Running practice without the bike is the correct way to prepare for joint bike trips. The leashed dog always has to stay even with the front wheel of the bicycle, so that you can keep an eye on your pet. It has to resist even the most inviting temptations along the route, such as other dogs, cats, wild game, the scent of game, or people it knows. The dog may endanger itself and the bicycle rider, if it tries to cross the road directly in front of the front wheel. To prevent such a disaster, always hold the leash in your hand in such a way that it can be dropped quickly if necessary, and never wind it around your wrist or tie it to the bike.

Note: Neither jogging nor running next to a bike can replace your dog's regular walk. That is the only way it can satisfy its need to gather information.

2) At first have your dog practice jumping over small logs.

3) Running beside a bike is good exercise for larger dogs.

Sports and Agility

Encouraging Your Pet to Participate

Dog sports can be a happy, meaningful form of recreation, a shared experience that encourages participation. They not only enrich the partnership between owner and pet, but also creates new ties and provide interesting contacts with like-minded people.

Sports as a Hobby

Engaging in dog sports can be an exciting hobby for you and your pet. Competition will fine-tune your dog's training and will also teach you new ways to work and play with it. Purebred dogs may participate and compete in several well-regulated activities sponsored by the American Kennel Club (AKC) and other organizations.

Conformation shows appeal to some dog fanciers. Dogs are judged according to standards established for individual breeds. The winners of the various breed competitions are awarded Best of Breed titles. Groups are made up of various breeds with similar characteristics, such as the hound group, sporting group, toy group, and others. The winners of breed competitions compete against other dogs of the same group for the Best of Group title. Then group winners compete for the Best in Show title. Although conformation exhibition is not really a sporting event, the animals shown must be very well trained in order to exhibit well and appeal to judges. Training a conformation dog is nearly as time-consuming as training an obedience trial dog.

Clearing the hurdle is easy, even for a dog that is not yet a perfect Agility athlete; jumping through a tire is more difficult.

Field trial competitions demonstrate a sporting dog's competency in performing the functions for which it was bred. Hunting dog owners must spend an enormous amount of time training their dogs for field trials. These dogs progress well beyond the fetch-and-carry games, and their natural instinctive talents are honed to fine edges. A winning field trial dog must possess talents in pointing, flushing, and retrieving, in addition to obedience and style. Titles awarded to winning field trial dogs are Amateur Field Champion and Field Champion.

Hunting tests are another type of competition for which sporting dogs may be trained. In competition, the winners may be awarded Junior Hunter, Senior Hunter, and Master Hunter titles.

Tracking tests are competitions in which dogs are judged according to their ability to follow trails by scent. Winners are awarded Tracking Dog, Tracking Dog Excellent, and Versatile Surface Tracking Dog titles.

AKC-Sponsored Events

Three obedience trial classes are sponsored by the AKC. The novice class winners accumulate points toward the Companion Dog title. Open classes earn points that will eventually confer the title of Companion Dog Excellent, and in the most advanced classes, dogs may earn the title Utility Dog. In all cases, the motives are to train the dogs to respond and react quickly and effectively to their owners' commands. Novice dogs work on and off leash and their tests are rather elementary. Open

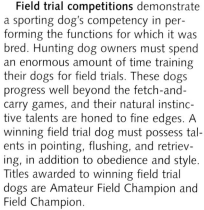

Some help from its human partner is in order when a dog is learning how to negotiate slalom poles.

classes are greater challenges since the dogs are entirely off leash, and their tests require more specialized training. In Utility classes, the degree of dogs' skill and education approach the ultimate; their natural instincts and mental capacity are put to full use.

Other Competitions

In addition to those official AKC events, many other competitions are devised and judged by the various all-breed and specialty dog clubs. They include weight-pulling contests, sled dog competitions, many specialized hunting events, rescue dog work, herding trials, and others. Many of these sporting events do not require AKC registration and are open to dogs of any type, providing they are properly obedience trained.

Agility Competition

Agility competitions are also becoming more popular in Europe and the United States. Agility competition, as the name implies, requires fitness and quick responses, mental, as well as physical. Dog and owner need to understand one another as implicitly as possible in order to traverse a maze of at least 12, and no more than 20, obstacles correctly and perfectly. The course includes hurdles, a wall, a table, a tire, a pipe tunnel, a fabric tunnel, a dog walk, and a moat. In addition, a broad jump, a seesaw, slalom poles, and an inclined wall are used. All make a wide variety of demands on the ability of the dog and on the relationship between the dog and its human partner. It is a timed event that is also judged by the dog's ability to negotiate obstacles as precisely as possible (see HOW-TO: Setting Up Agility Obstacles, page 54).

Almost All Dogs Can Do Agility

Good prerequisites for an agility winner are medium size, an active nature, well-angled hindquarters, quickness, an enjoyment of jumping, a sure eye for distance and height, quick reactions, and perfect basic training. In addition, trust and a close bond between owner and pet are necessary. In principle, you can embark upon the agility adventure with any dog, with the possible exception of breeds whose physical conformation does not lend itself to athletic activities. Such breeds include basset hounds, dachshunds, Skye terriers, bulldogs, pugs, Saint Bernards, and dogs whose hindquarters are not properly angled.

Agility Titles

AKC: The American Kennel Club (AKC) held its first agility competition on August 11, 1994 in Houston, Texas. Over 190 dogs of 58 different breeds competed. Since then, AKC agility trials have been held all over the country and more and more dogs are competing—dogs of all sizes and breeds.

The AKC offers three levels of competition, each giving the dog and owner a chance to earn a title. In the novice class, dogs can earn a Novice Agility title. After earning that, the dogs move on to the open class where they can earn the Open Agility title; from the excellent class, dogs can earn the Agility Excellent title. In addition, dogs that have earned the Agility Excellent title may continue to compete and eventually earn the Master Agility Excellent title.

For a copy of the AKC's competition rules, write to: AKC, 51 Madison Avenue, New York, New York 10010.

USDAA: The United States Dog Agility Association (USDAA) was formed in 1986 to promote the sport of dog agility. Recognizing the appeal of this activity, the USDAA stresses community and family involvement, inviting spectators to watch and cheer for their favorite canine athlete and offering a way for the entire family to spend quality time with their pet. The USDAA's junior handler programs invite children's participation.

The USDAA sponsors numerous competitions at which dogs and owners can earn a variety of titles. Titles that children and their dogs can earn through the junior handler program include: Junior Handler Beginner Agility, Junior Handler Elementary Agility, Junior Handler Intermediate Agility and Junior Handler Senior Agility. Adults and their dogs can compete and earn the following titles: Agility Dog, Advanced Agility Dog, Master Agility Dog, and Agility Dog Champion.

Write to the USDAA for a copy of the competition regulations at: USDAA, PO Box 850955, Richardson, Texas 75085-0955.

Other groups: Several other groups offer agility competitions and award titles for performance. The Australian Shepherd Club of America (ASCA) offers competitions for all breeds of dogs, not just Australian Shepherds. The club's agility program is very similar to that of the AKC. For competition rules and regulations, as well as information about clubs sponsoring competitions, write to: ASCA, 6091 East State Highway 21, Bryan, Texas 77808-9652.

The United Kennel Club offers all-breed competition, too. The UKC's program was established by Bud Kramer, a pioneer in agility in the United States. He and his friend Bob Self were both very interested in obedience training and competition when they were first introduced to the sport of agility in England, where agility was very much a spectator sport and was patterned after equestrian jumping contests. The jumps were very high and only the dogs that could clear the jumps and run very fast could participate. Since Kramer wanted all dogs to have fun with agility, a program was started in the United States that was open to all dogs. Eventually, after much revision and reorganization, the program was adopted by the UKC. For more information about the UKC program, write to: UKC, 100 East Kilgore Road, Kalamazoo, Michigan 49001-5598.

Before Entering Agility Competitions

There are several things you should know before entering an agility competition.

1. Make sure you have a copy of the group's competition rules. If you have questions about the rules, call the organization.

2. Make sure your dog has trained on the same type of obstacles on which it will be competing. If your dog will be required to run through several tunnels, jump over numerous hurdles, and walk over a sway bridge, make sure it has had a chance to train on those same types of obstacles. If it

hasn't, contact a dog trainer in your area. If the trainer doesn't have any agility obstacles, he or she will know who does.

It is not enough that your dog is familiar with the obstacles, it must also know how to do them properly. Many obstacles must be done in a certain manner. For example, all of the obstacles that have ramps—such as the A-frame, seesaw, dog walk, and sway bridge—have contact zones. Contact zones are painted areas at the base of the ramps and are there to prevent the dog from jumping off the obstacle too soon. Each dog must touch at least one paw into each contact zone.

An important exercise in tournament sports is heeling free (off leash).

Be careful on the seesaw until the tipping point is reached.

3. Make sure your dog's obedience training is up to par. Because your dog will be working off leash in very distracting circumstances, make sure you have trained it so that it is ready. Your dog should have a quick response to your *come* command every time you call, no matter what is going on around it.

What Is Competition Like?

Each agility competition course will be set up differently. The obstacles will be in a different order or pattern. Approaches to obstacles may be straight on, they may be curved to the right or left, or the approach may even be a sharp turn. Obstacles may be close together or spread out. The approach to one obstacle may be very close to the approach to another obstacle.

Prior to starting the competition, you will be allowed to walk through the course. Make sure you walk through as if your dog were by your side. How would you direct your dog? What commands? What hand signals? Where will you be in relation to your dog? If you can work these things out prior to starting with your dog, you can save time and confusion.

In agility competition, the dog must run, off leash, over each obstacle as quickly as possible, and then dash across the finish line. During this, you will be directing the dog over a preset course so that the dog is doing each obstacle in its correct order. Also, the dog must go over or through each obstacle correctly. When all of these things are done, the fastest dog wins.

On the way down, the red contact zone has to be touched.

Noncompetitive Agility

Agility does not have to be a competitive sport. Although many people (and their dogs!) enjoy competition, not all dogs are created equal when it comes to agility. Golden retrievers, Labrador retrievers, Border collies, and Australian shepherds are athletic, quick, and agile, and do very well in the sport. Basset hounds, clumber spaniels, and mastiffs may have fun on the course, but may not be as fast or agile as some other breeds. However, just because some dogs are not competitive doesn't mean that they cannot have fun with agility.

Many dog trainers, dog obedience instructors, and dog training clubs use agility as part of their training program.

For young dogs and puppies, agility helps teach body awareness, coordination, and confidence. Even ten-week-old puppies can learn to navigate some of the easier obstacles, especially when motivated by food treats. Agility also teaches the dog to trust the owner, that if the owner says, "Let's climb this obstacle!" the dog can do it and the owner will make sure that it is a positive experience.

Some dog training clubs will set up an agility course for the dog-owning public. After paying a minimal fee, dog owners can take their dog through the course while a supervising club member explains the obstacles and helps dog owners teach their dog. For a course near you, call your local dog trainer or dog training club.

HOW-TO:
Setting Up Agility Obstacles

The different organizations sponsoring agility competitions each have their own rules and regulations pertaining to the sport. However, the rules are similar enough that dogs can be easily trained to compete with each of the different groups.

Jump Heights

Many of the obstacles in agility require the dogs to jump. The jumps are set at predetermined heights, based upon the height of the dog at the point of the shoulder.

The AKC has established jump heights divisions as follows:
• Dogs 10 inches tall at the shoulder and smaller will jump 8 inches.
• Dogs over 10 inches but smaller than 14 inches at the shoulder, will jump 12 inches.
• Dogs between 14 and 18 inches will jump 16 inches.
• Dogs between 18 and 22 inches will jump 20 inches.
• Dogs over 22 inches will jump 24 inches.

Double Bar Jump

The double bar jump consists of two parallel bars, one in front of the other, positioned at the correct height for the dog. The dog is to jump both bars at the same time, without touching the ground in between. The distance between the two bars is one half the height of the jump.

Tire Jump

The tire jump consists of a tire (usually a motorcycle tire) mounted in a frame. The frame should be at least 48 inches square with the tire hung inside the square. The height of the tire must be adjustable to the various jump heights. The dog is to jump through the center of the tire.

Window Jump

The window jump opening is 24 inches square, hung in a 48-inch-square frame. The window must be adjustable, up and down, to the various jump heights. The dog jumps through the open window.

Broad Jump

The broad jump is comprised of several flat planks of ascending sizes. The smallest would be 6 inches wide, by 4 feet long, on 2-inch legs. The largest would be 8 inches wide, by 5 feet long, on 6-inch legs. Set side by side in ascending size, the jump can spread from 16 inches wide (for the smallest dogs) to 48 inches wide (for the largest dogs). The distance each dog must jump is twice what the dog would jump over a high jump.

A-Frame

The A-frame is made of two wood panels (or sheets of exterior plywood) that are 4 feet wide by 8 feet long. They are attached at the top and opened to an A-frame (pyramid) shape. At the peak, the A-frame should be 5 feet tall. The A-frame is finished with a nonskid surface, as well as slats placed every 12 inches to give additional traction. The dog must climb up the A-frame and back down the other side, without jumping off the obstacle.

Dog Walk

The dog walk consists of an elevated plank that is much like a gymnast's balance beam, except that there is a ramp on one end for the dog to walk up

and a ramp on the other end for the dog to walk down. All planks are 12 inches wide and 8 feet long. The center plank is 3 feet high. The planks are finished with a nonskid surface. The dog must walk (or run) up one ramp, go across the center section, and descend the other ramp, without jumping off.

Seesaw

The seesaw looks like one found in a child's playground. It consists of a plank 12 inches wide by 12 feet long. A 24-inch-tall base anchors the plank and acts as a fulcrum. The dog walks up one end of the planks, reaches the balance point, causing the other end of the plank to move toward the ground, and then walks off that lowered end. The dog is not to jump off while the end of the plank is still in the air.

Pause Table

The pause table is a 36-inch-square sturdy table or box. The dog is to jump up on the table

and either sit or lie down. The dog cannot jump off the table until directed to leave by you.

Weave Poles

The weave poles are 36 inches tall by 1 inch in diameter. There are between 6 and 12 poles that are mounted at the base, set about 24 inches apart. The dog is to weave through the poles, in and out, without missing any poles.

Open Tunnel

The open tunnel is made of flexible material that can be curved or straightened. The tunnel is 24 inches in diameter and 10 to 20 feet long, and should be anchored so that it doesn't roll or move. It is set up so that the dog cannot see the other open end. The dog runs into one end, through the tunnel, and out the other end.

Closed Tunnel

The closed tunnel has a rigid entrance section with a flexible cloth tunnel attached to it. The

entrance section is 24 inches in diameter. The cloth section is attached to the entrance section and flares to 96 inches in circumference. The total length of the cloth chute should be 12 to 15 feet. The dog is to run into the entrance and push its way through the closed chute.

Crawl Tunnel

The crawl tunnel is 24 inches wide and 6 feet long. The top is adjustable to raise and lower so that it can be set to the jump heights appropriate for the particular dog.

Sway Bridge

The sway bridge is a flexible bridge that is 24 inches wide by 8 feet long, raised to a height of 3 feet. The ramps on either side of the bridge are 24 inches wide by 6 feet long, slatted every 12 inches, and covered with a nonskid surface. The dog is to run up one ramp, cross the bridge, and run back down the ramp on the other side.

Some agility obstacles (from left to right):
1) double bar
2) A-frame
3) pause table
4) tire
5) dog walk
6) tunnel

The dog should not be allowed to jump off the side of the inclined wall.

Proper Nutrition for Your Athlete

Fitness Starts with Your Dog's Food

Anyone who exercises needs strength. Dogs engaged in sports competition require a diet that is nutritionally balanced and palatable. Only animals that are regularly asked to perform competitively at a high level actually have an increased energy requirement, however. That applies to herding dogs, hunting dogs, guard dogs, sled dogs, and racing dogs in training and competition. The total daily caloric requirement may double in dogs during heavy work or training.

The nutritional needs of a family dog, on the other hand, change very little when it takes part in recreational sports and games. Nevertheless, feeding your pet the right foods in the proper balance is the basis of its physical fitness. Among the factors you need to consider when establishing its diet are the intensity and frequency of your pet's training, its age, physical condition, and the size of the dog.

If you think your pet is over-worked, don't let sympathy lead you to give it extra food on a regular basis: Unless weight loss is noted, extra food will cause obesity.

The "Figure Test"

You can easily tell whether your dog is too fat by conducting a "figure test." Behind its shoulders and about midway up its chest, try to feel its ribs. If you cannot feel them, your pet is over-weight.

Nutritional Check

You need to check regularly—especially at the start of training—to see whether your dog is being fed properly and adequately. Look for these things:
• Constant body weight: Weigh the dog once a month.
• Normal stool: The stool should be neither too firm nor too soft.
• Supple skin and glossy coat: Dry skin and a shaggy coat often are signs of nutritional deficiencies due to an unbalanced diet.
• Good appetite: Occasional lack of appetite is no reason for concern, and there are many different causes. If it continues to refuse food for more than 48 hours, however, consult your veterinarian.

No Results without Water

Drinking water is equally important for your dog's physical fitness. The normal body temperature of a dog (between 100.4 and 102.2°F [38–39°C]) rises relatively quickly during strenuous activity, depending on the day's temperature, the relative humidity, and the thickness of the dog's coat. If it rises above 105.8°F (41°C), the dog will lose its ability to perform. Water consumption is critical to prevent overheating. A dog's body heat dissipates through the tongue when the dog pants and through sweat glands located in several body areas. Unlike humans, dogs do not perspire freely, and perspiration does not adequately cool them.

A properly nourished dog that gets plenty of diversion and exercise through sports and games will clearly show how well it feels.

Feeding Puppies and Young Dogs

When feeding puppies and half-grown dogs, consider their rapid growth. Young animals are typically very active. Early training in sports and games should not be too strenuous for young dogs, but should act as a way of carefully guiding their natural desire for exercise. Consequently, there is no need to give them extra food to compensate for the energy expended in play. Overfeeding puppies can be quite dangerous, because growth and weight gain are accelerated unduly. Larger breeds in particular may develop skeletal problems as a result of dietary imbalances or overfeeding.

Most commercial dog foods formulated for puppies and young dogs contain all the essential nutrients, vitamins, and minerals. The recommended feeding amounts on the label should under no circumstances be exceeded, even if your pet romps extensively and regularly in your yard. And remember: After every meal, your pet needs to rest at least one hour before resuming play!

Adult Dogs: The Mix Makes the Difference

Premium-quality commercial dog foods, whether canned, semimoist, or dry, contain everything your dog needs for a healthy diet. If using dry food, make sure your pet gets enough water.

If your dog plays sports and games for recreation and exercise, its energy requirements do not increase. The usual amount of food is sufficient unless weight loss is noted.

High-Energy Foods

Performance animals engaged in stressful training or working situations

Feeding Rules

Animals that are used in competition reach their performance peak no sooner than six hours after their last meal. There are some rules for feeding your dog that are absolutely critical:

• Be especially careful with large breeds. There is a risk of a life-threatening gastric torsion (see page 59) if the dog is extremely active after being fed. My recommendation is to spread out the daily ration over two or three meals.

• Drinking water always needs to be available during games and sports as well.

• From the outset, adhere to fixed feeding times. Remove food if not eaten within 30 minutes. Food left out attracts insects, and contaminated food can be dangerous to the health of the animal. During training too, stick to whatever feeding system you have set up.

• Tidbits like dog biscuits or crackers used as rewards should be given immediately after each successful performance. For the dog, it is principally its owner's praise that counts. The treat does not need to be a high-energy, full-scale snack between meals.

• "Play foods," such as bones made of rawhide or hard biscuits are an ideal way to stimulate the dog's play instinct and an important means of strengthening its masticatory muscles, as well as helping to keep its teeth clean.

require high-energy foods. Sled dogs, sporting dogs, utility dogs, and others will benefit from special diets but do not attempt to formulate high-energy diets without professional guidance. It is usually best to obtain special working dog diets that have been scientifically prepared for those animals. Such diets are available from pet supply stores and veterinarians.

A common mistake made by novice owners is to add cheese, meat, or eggs to an animal's diet to increase the protein. Protein increase is not always beneficial, and can actually be dangerous. All natural meat, dairy, and egg products also contain fat, and without a complete analysis, their actual makeup is unknown. It is better to let the dog food manufacturers formulate your dog's food. With their scientists, laboratories, feeding trials, and experience, they are more qualified to formulate stress diets.

Premium commercial high-energy diets usually contain more fat than is found in maintenance diets. More important than quantity, however, is the quality of ingredients and the balance between ingredients. Those special diets also have added vitamin and mineral elements to assure proper utilization of the food.

Older Dogs: Easy-to-Digest Foods and Light Exercise

Depending on its breed, a dog begins to show old-age signs after it is seven or eight years old. It exhibits markedly less desire for exercise, and its energy requirement drops by about 20 percent. If its appetite remains unchanged, it may become obese.

Games and sports, combined with a decrease in the amount of food, can put a stop to weight gain. In addition to easily digestible, low-energy foods, an older dog needs light exercise (see page 11).

Training with senior dogs is not directed at high performance; rather, it is intended to have a therapeutic effect. Light, regular exercise keeps them vital,

Drinking water is absolutely essential for a canine athlete, to keep it from getting overheated.

revives their spirits, distracts them from the aches and pains of old age, strengthens their self-confidence, and gives them increased pep.

Resting after Meals

Make sure that your pet rests for at least one hour before resuming play after a meal. This is absolutely essential with large breeds in particular, since they could develop gastric torsion.

Gastric Torsion

The symptoms of gastric torsion are upper abdominal bloating, gagging and drooling, difficulty breathing, and restlessness. As the bloat develops, the stomach is pulled upward. The food-filled portion of the stomach, by contrast, sags downward. As a result, the stomach rotates on its longitudinal axis, interrupting the blood supply to the stomach. This leads to death in a few hours.

When the first symptoms appear, the dog should immediately be taken to the veterinarian. Surgical connection of the twisted stomach is usually possible if diagnosed and treated quickly.

Index

Useful Addresses and Literature

Associations and Clubs

American Kennel Club (AKC)
51 Madison Ave
New York, NY 10010

United Kennel Club (UKC)
100 East Kilgore Road
Kalamazoo, MI 49001-5598

United States Dog Agility
Association (USDAA)
PO Box 850955
Richardson, TX 75085-0955

Books

Baer, Ted. *Communicating with Your Dog.* Barron's Educational Series, Inc., Hauppauge, New York: 1989.

————. *How to Teach Your Old Dog New Tricks.* Barron's Educational Series, Inc., Hauppauge, New York: 1991.

Frye, Fredric L. *First Aid for Your Dog.* Barron's Educational Series, Inc., Hauppauge, New York: 1989.

Schlegl-Kofler, Katharina. *Educating Your Dog.* Barron's Educational Series, Inc., Hauppauge, New York: 1996.

About the Author

Dr. Gerd Ludwig has a degree in zoology, with an emphasis on anthropology, ethology, and evolution studies. He is an editor of the magazine *Das Tier.*

About the Photographer

Christine Steimer has been a freelance photographer since 1985; she has specialized in photographing animals since 1989. She is responsible for the photographs in several pet owner's manuals published by Barron's. Her work appears regularly in *Das Tier.*

About the Illustrator

Renate Holzner works as a freelance illustrator in Germany. Her broad repertoire extends from line drawings through illustrations in the style of photorealism to computer graphics.

Resting between games is imperative.

Acknowledgments

The author and the publishers of this book are grateful to Dr. Volker Hach, a veterinary surgeon in Frankfurt, for providing important information found in "Tips from the Veterinarian" and "Proper Nutrition for Your Athlete." Special thanks go to our consulting editors: Dan Rice, D.V.M., for suggesting ways to make this mook more appropriate for our American readers, and Liz Palika, columnist on sports and agility for *Dog Fancy* magazine, for providing the section on agility competition in the United States.

© Copyright 1996 by Barron's Educational Series, Inc.

All inquiries should be addressed to:
Barron's Educational Series, Inc.
250 Wireless Boulevard
Hauppauge, NY 11788

International Standard Book No. 0-8120-9721-1

Library of Congress Catalog Card No. 96-19484

Library of Congress Cataloging-in-Publication Data
Ludwig, Gerd.
      [*Mitdem Hund Spielen un Trainieren.* English]
      Fun and games with your dog / by Gerd Ludwig ; consulting editor, Dan Rice.
            p.   cm.
      Includes bibliographical references (p.   ) and index.
      ISBN 0-8120-9721-1
            1. Games for dogs. 2. Dogs. I. Rice, Dan, 1933–   . II. Title.
SF427.45.L8413   1996
636.7'0887—dc20   96-19484
                                                                      CIP

Printed in Hong Kong

9876543

Important Note

This Barron's pet owner's guide deals with games and sports for dogs. The author and the publisher think it is important to point out that all the information on training, designing exercises, and planning games and sports is intended for owners of healthy animals. In this guide, only marginal attention can be given to the specific requirements for risk-free play with young, old, or sick dogs. Please design exercise programs for such dogs only in consultation with your veterinarian or an experienced training supervisor in your dog sports club.

We urge you to purchase liability insurance for all dogs that engage in sports. Only such a policy will offer adequate coverage in case of damage to someone else's property or accidents.

Large balloons in many colors can give a puppy a good scare when one or more of them pop with a loud bang. Even for young dogs, however, it's all a matter of getting used to things.